Regaining Your Happiness in Seven Weeks

A Training Program

by *Jonathan Lockwood Huie*

Copyright © 2010 by Jonathan Lockwood Huie.
All rights reserved.

ISBN: 9781453795132

Jonathan Lockwood Huie
www.DreamThisDay.com
www.JonathanLockwoodHuie.com
jlh@jlhuie.com

Regaining Your Happiness in Seven Weeks

About the Author

Jonathan Lockwood Huie, consultant, speaker, personal coach, and lover of life is known as "The Philosopher of Happiness."

Mr. Huie writes the popular *Daily Inspiration - Daily Quote* which is available on-line at **www.DreamThisDay.com** and via free email subscription.

For 30 years, Mr. Huie was a highly successful technologist and executive of Silicon Valley start-up companies, bearing titles such as Senior Vice President and Chief Architect. After one of his start-ups was acquired in 2000, Jonathan directed his attention toward the human issues of happiness, life satisfaction, work-life balance, and cooperative behavior (teamwork).

Mr. Huie is pleased to receive your email at jlh@jlhuie.com

Jonathan Lockwood Huie
www.DreamThisDay.com
www.JonathanLockwoodHuie.com
jlh@jlhuie.com

Also by Jonathan Lockwood Huie

100 Secrets for Living a Life You Love:
Finding Happiness Despite Life's Roadblocks
www.dreamthisday.com/secrets-life-love

Simply An Inspired Life:
Consciously Choosing Unbounded Happiness in Good Times and Bad
- co-authored with Mary Anne Radmacher - Conari Press 2009.
www.SimplyAnInspiredLife.com

Daily Inspiration - Daily Quote
Sign-up at www.DreamThisDay.com to receive Jonathan's *Daily Inspiration - Daily Quote* free via email.

Regaining Your Happiness in Seven Weeks

Table of Contents

Introduction 1
Week 1 Day 1: Observing The World - Gossip and Complain 3
Week 1 Day 2: Observing The World - Stress, Anger, and Fear 5
Week 1 Day 3: Observing The World - Staying Alert 8
Week 1 Day 4: Observing The World - It Hurts Just To Listen 10
Week 1 Day 5: Observing The World - Our Stories 12
Week 1 Day 6: Observing The World - Happier Stories 14
Week 1 Day 7: Observing The World - Go Crazy With Stories 15
Week 2 Day 1: Observing Family and Friends - Belonging 16
Week 2 Day 2: Observing Family and Friends - Approval 17
Week 2 Day 3: Observing Family and Friends - Judgments 18
Week 2 Day 4: Observing Family and Friends - Open Heart 20
Week 2 Day 5: Observing Family and Friends - Life Is A Mirror 22
Week 2 Day 6: Observing Family and Friends - Perspective 25
Week 2 Day 7: Observing Family and Friends - Dance Lightly 27
Week 3 Day 1: Observing Myself - Silence and Solitude 30
Week 3 Day 2: Observing Myself - I Am the Wizard 33
Week 3 Day 3: Observing Myself - I Choose My World 35
Week 3 Day 4: Observing Myself - Up Is Down & Down Is Up 38
Week 3 Day 5: Observing Myself - My Hate Hurts Me Most 40
Week 3 Day 6: Observing Myself - My Teachers 43
Week 3 Day 7: Observing Myself - Peace, Ultimate Blessing 47
Week 4 Day 1: Observing My Interactions - Would I Do *That*? 48
Week 4 Day 2: Observing My Interactions - Importance 50
Week 4 Day 3: Observing My Interactions - Why, Why, Why? 52
Week 4 Day 4: Observing My Interactions - Complaints 54
Week 4 Day 5: Observing My Interactions - Thoughts 56
Week 4 Day 6: Observing My Interactions - Expectations 58

Week 4 Day 7: Observing My Interactions - Forgiveness 60
Week 5 Day 1: Accepting My Past - Early Childhood 64
Week 5 Day 2: Accepting My Past - Adolescence 67
Week 5 Day 3: Accepting My Past - On My Own 68
Week 5 Day 4: Accepting My Past - Adult Issues....................................... 69
Week 5 Day 5: Accepting My Past - Owning My Shadows 71
Week 5 Day 6: Accepting My Past - Un-Learning & Re-Training................. 72
Week 5 Day 7: Accepting My Past - Loving My Real Self............................ 74
Week 6 Day 1: Transformation - Overcoming My Fears 76
Week 6 Day 2: Transformation - Releasing Anger 78
Week 6 Day 3: Transformation - Problems Are Illusions 81
Week 6 Day 4: Transformation - Accepting Miraculous Gifts 82
Week 6 Day 5: Transformation - The End Of Suffering................................ 84
Week 6 Day 6: Transformation - Don't Believe Anything............................. 85
Week 6 Day 7: Transformation - Let The Light In.. 87
Week 7 Day 1: The Future - Life Is A Grand Adventure 90
Week 7 Day 2: The Future - Just Do It with Courage 92
Week 7 Day 3: The Future - The Power Of My Word 94
Week 7 Day 4: The Future - Think Outside the Box..................................... 95
Week 7 Day 5: The Future - Powerful Dreams & Action 97
Week 7 Day 6: The Future - Everything Is One 99
Week 7 Day 7: The Future - Life Is a PERFECT Mess 100
Conclusion - What's Next? 102

Regaining Your Happiness in Seven Weeks

Regaining Your Happiness in Seven Weeks

A Training Program

The writings of Jonathan Lockwood Huie are based solely upon his life experiences and are his opinions. Consult an appropriate medical professional for any issues of physical or emotional health.

Regaining Your Happiness in Seven Weeks

Introduction

The *Regaining Your Happiness in Seven Weeks* Training Program is designed to reduce your emotional suffering and increase the joy you find in everyday living by helping you to:

1. Understand the role your past plays in triggering your current emotional state.
2. Access the power of forgiveness and gratitude to create happiness.
3. Establish a framework for designing your inspired future.

Each of the 49 Daily Lessons of this program consists of a concise insight into that day's issue and one or more exercises to give life to that insight during the course of your normal daily activities.

> *Try not to have a good time... this is supposed to be educational.*
> *- Charles M. Schulz*

Our purpose for the next seven weeks is to transform into a person with consistent access to joy and serenity - a happy, contented person. To do this, you are going to have to break some lifelong habits that are holding you back. But these habits are so ingrained - so much a part of you - that you can't even see these habits in yourself. Further, if a well meaning friend pointed out one of these habits, you would most likely react with disbelief, and possibly anger.

If you can't see these habits in yourself, and rebel if someone points them out, it looks like you're stuck, right? Fortunately not! The trick to breaking through, is to start by observing other people.

The early lessons focus on observing other people, and learning to identify what those people are doing to destroy their peace and happiness. We're going to watch and listen to enough other people to see the patterns of self-destruction. While everyone is different, all humans share some very well defined patterns of emotionally self destructive behavior.

Once we can see that everyone we observe shares these self-destructive behaviors, it will be time to hold up a mirror to ourselves and consider the possibility that, as a member of the human race, we might just possibly share these same self-destructive behaviors.

This is an intensive training program. Training is very different from teaching. Teaching is what happens in a physics class or an English lit class. Training is what a sports coach does. When you are being trained in golf, for example, you don't focus on learning the physics of action-reaction; and you don't focus on the history of the game of golf. Rather, you get trained by having your coach position your body, guide your swing, and watch over you as you hit bucket after bucket of practice balls until your body bypasses your mind, your great swing feels natural every time, and whenever you sleep, your dreams are of hitting golf balls.

Training often doesn't make sense to the participant. Think of the football coach who insists his players run sprints for two weeks before they even see a football; or the great "wax-on, wax-off" scene from the movie *Karate Kid* in which the karate teacher trains the young man in hand strength and coordination by waxing the teacher's car. Like the "karate kid", sometimes we can best be trained by trusting the trainer and accepting each day's training.

Please commit forty nine days to this training. Each day's insights and exercise build upon the previous day. The impact will be greatest if you don't know what is coming next, so don't read ahead.

The heart of this training course is the **Today In My World** exercises. Don't cheat yourself by giving even one of these daily exercises less than your full attention.

By the time you're done, your very instincts are going to be altered. You will have a very different reaction to getting cut off in traffic, being late for an appointment, or watching the latest tragedy on the nightly news.

Thank you for joining me in this journey we call life,
   Jonathan

Jonathan Lockwood Huie
www.DreamThisDay.com   www.JonathanLockwoodHuie.com   jlh@jlhuie.com

Week 1 Day 1: Observing The World - Gossip and Complain

From the errors of others, a wise man corrects his own.
- Publilius Syrus

It's just gossip, you know. Gossip is the new pornography.
- the Woody Allen movie Manhattan

I feel that if a person can't communicate, the very least he can do is to shut up.
- Tom Lehrer

We are going to begin this seven week Happiness e-Training program not by looking at ourselves, but by observing those we do not even know.

Why do we not begin with ourselves? We are too emotionally involved with our own lives to be able to observe ourselves objectively and to learn. We will begin by observing those we do not know, then move to observing friends and family, and finally, in the third week, we will move to observing ourselves.

Are you dreading that family get-together or office party? You just know that uncle Harry is going to give you his opinion of politics for three hours, and that Joyce is going to put down every dress in the room. You can stay home, you can just suffer through it, or you can have a good laugh labeling the behaviors.

Stereotyping people may not be considered nice, but there really are personality types, and nothing brings that out like a holiday gathering. Do you know these people:

The Opinion: the man or woman who knows exactly how the world should behave. "If I were President, I'd fix this economy right away by ..." "They shouldn't let dogs bark. I've called the sheriff six times on the guy across the street."

The Know-It-All: The Know-it-all is very different from the Opinion - he or she really does know something useful about everything. It's unsettling - it's embarrassing - it feels a little like watching one of those quiz shows where "people picked from our audience" know the answers to amazing trivia questions. We wonder if the quiz show is faked, but this person is standing right in front of us.

The Bully: "The next time my neighbor's dog barks, I'm going to go over there and pound him." "I've got three guns, so nobody better mess with me." "If there's a scratch on my Harley, somebody's history."

The Sob Story: You just know that something terrible has happened to them since the last time you talked to them - even if that was yesterday. The Sob Story can't keep a job or a romantic interest. Their car is always in the shop or about to be repossessed. How can that much bad luck attend any one person?

The Storm Cloud: Joe Btfsplk was a character in Al Capp's Li'l Abner cartoon strip. Joe walked around with a dark cloud over his head. Although Joe was a happy person and loving friend, trouble always followed Joe. If Joe was there, an earthquake, tornado, or swarm of locusts was sure to follow.

The Perfect Life: The perfect job, the perfect spouse, the perfect kids. Never a wrinkle, never a hair out of place. Gag me with a spoon I'm so jealous.

The Egomaniac: No one else exists in the life of the Egomaniac. I did this, and I want that, and pooh on the rest of you.

The Gossip: everything you didn't want to know about Mary's arthritis and Joe's love life.

The Undresser: No, not the stripper, or the streaker, or the lecher - the Undresser is the person who takes apart everyone's wardrobe piece by piece. "She should never have worn those shoes with that dress." "How could she let him leave the house in that shirt."

After you have finished laughing at them, have compassion for all these people. Some - like The Sob Story and The Bully are constantly suffering. The others are generally unaware of how much their behaviors push everyone away.

Today In My World: If it's convenient, spend an hour today in a busy coffee house - alone. Otherwise, just pay attention to the strangers you encounter today - at a restaurant, at a bar, at the bank, in the grocery store, on the subway, at your job (remember that we're observing people we haven't met before). Note everything you see and hear someone do or say that doesn't appear to be in the best interest of that person. How do you feel when you hear their gossip and complaints?

Week 1 Day 2: Observing The World - Stress, Anger, and Fear

As far as we can discern, the sole purpose of human existence is to kindle a light in the darkness of mere being.
- Carl Jung

Speech is the mirror of the soul; as a man speaks, so is he.
- Publilius Syrus

Human beings are perceivers, but the world that they perceive is an illusion.
- Carlos Castaneda

Let me bring peace into moments of chaos.
- jlh (Jonathan Lockwood Huie)

How often we have times that try our patience and our sanity. Our boss is having an angry day and makes unreasonable demands. The driver in the next lane gives us the finger. Our neighbor rants how if he ran the town, he would just kill off all the dogs and cats, and if he were president, he would just bomb all the SOBs. Our instinctive reaction is to get angry and fight back.

In times like that, pause, and consider how life looks to that other individual. Although they are acting belligerent, in truth they are very much afraid of life. In their reality, life is a dangerous and fearful undertaking, and their instinct is to respond aggressively to that perceived danger.

At such times, consider breathing deeply and slowly, and thinking compassionate thoughts about that person. If it fits your belief system, pray for the anger, pain, hatred, and fear to be washed from their souls. If it fits your belief system, have an intention for their well-being, and send them healing energy. Whatever your belief system, know that they are troubled and wish inner-peace for them.

I strongly recommend that you express your prayers and intentions silently. Saying openly to an angry person, "I pray for you to receive inner-peace." is almost certain to provoke an even angrier reaction.

By establishing a compassionate intention toward an angry person, you can then maintain your own inner peace as you interact with them.

Being angry is as close as a human being can come to experiencing hell on earth.
- jlh

Anger is something that each one of us has experienced - some of us only occasionally, some almost daily. Can we eliminate all anger? Probably not. We will always have expectations, and those expectations will often be unmet.

Disappointment is the principle cause of anger. When we are disappointed, we look for someone to blame. Declaring someone to be *at fault* is the nature of anger. Anger is always directed at *someone* - possibly God or the non-specific *they*, but some animate entity.

You've told yourself a hundred times that you aren't going to get angry - really angry - ever again, but wham, you start to feel that telltale heat, locked shoulders, clenched jaw, shallow breathing. Someone has just done something really awful and you are *angry* at them. What now?

Here are 7 Secrets to Stop Anger before It Stops You:

1. Recognize when you are angry: It may not immediately occur to you that you are angry. You know that you have been wronged, and you can see everyone around you take a step back, but especially if you are really angry, it may take a while to gain the clarity to acknowledge your anger. Anger clouds perception and thinking, so make a special effort to spot it early and put it into words, "I am angry."

2. Breathe deeply: Concentrate on taking slow deep breaths. Sometimes this is all it takes to break out of anger and gain clarity on the issue. At other times, breathing deeply is just a beginning, but it paves the way for the rest of the secrets.

3. Focus your anger: Get clear *what* you are angry about and *who* you are angry at. Talk to yourself, "I am angry at Joe because he ..." Don't let your anger expand onto innocent bystanders, especially those trying to help calm you down. Don't refocus your anger onto everything that Joe has ever done or failed to do.

4. Remember that you are in charge: Anger is an expression of frustration and helplessness. Remember that you always have options - you can design your own life. No one can steal your happiness - unless you let them.

5. Look for the silver lining: There is a silver lining to every disappointment. Your boss fired you and you are furious. Probably it was a blessing. Now you have the opportunity to get a better job that you really enjoy.

6. Consider forgiveness: Angry and happy don't mix. Flush out the angry, and the happy has a place to put down roots. Forgive everyone for everything in order to give anger and resentment a chance to fade. Forgive and you can become happy. Forgiving is not a gift to someone else - Forgiving is our gift to ourselves - a great gift - the gift of happiness.

7. Accept that Life is NOT "Supposed to be Fair": Know that there is no single way that life is "supposed" to be. Demanding that life meet our expectations is a sure fire recipe for a miserable existence. Life is a game with no rules. Life just happens to us regardless of our best intentions. To choose happiness, be open to receiving whatever life throws at you - with Gratitude. Have NO Expectations of life.

Today In My World: Spend some time today at a table for one at a busy coffee house, if possible. Otherwise, just observe people you don't know. How do they look - attentive? eye contact? preoccupied? How do they sound - stressed? or calm? afraid? angry? How do you feel when you sense their stress and hear their anger or fear?

Week 1 Day 3: Observing The World - Staying Alert

The voyage of discovery is not in seeking new landscapes but in having new eyes.
- Marcel Proust

The question is not what you look at, but what you see.
- Henry David Thoreau

The most pathetic person in the world is someone who has sight, but no vision.
- Helen Keller

To be surprised, to wonder, is to begin to understand.
- Jose Ortega Y Gasset

"What we've got here is failure to communicate."
- the movie Cool Hand Luke

The invariable mark of wisdom is to see the miraculous in the common.
- Ralph Waldo Emerson

Normally, we do not so much look at things as overlook them.
- Alan Watts

Every day is a new beginning - a day for a new plan and new action. If today, in conscious awareness, you choose the same plan as yesterday, you are wise. If you choose a different plan, you are equally wise. Whatever you choose, choose with intention.

Be Here Now.
- Ram Dass

Three little words, but a world of wisdom. Behind that simple saying is both the call to live in the moment and also to live consciously. Often people go through life in a sort of fog - unhappy, helpless to address the unhappiness, and unhappy about the helpless feeling. Life cannot be lived fully or joyfully if our thoughts are focused on regretting the past, preoccupied with anticipating the future, or lost in the mind-fog of unconscious habitual behavior.

Mind fog can be addressed in two steps, the first of the mind, the second of the heart.

1. Have a talk with your mind (it really is something separate from yourself). Lay down the law. "My life begins TODAY. I am like a newborn. I have what I have today; I have my fingers, my toes, some people in my life, some material and financial state. Yesterday is only a dream - perhaps a nightmare, perhaps a cherished

memory, but only a dream - nothing more. I will make all decisions and actions based solely on what I have today as a starting point." Personalize your conversation with your mind and be clear that you just won't tolerate any thoughts or actions that are not based on today's facts.

2. Moving to your heart, Breathe. Close your eyes and breathe deeply - slowly - fill your lungs with love and gratitude - exhale each and every trouble - again and again - gratitude in, troubles out. Speak to your self from your heart as you would to a newborn baby, "I love you because I love you. You are a part of me, and I need no reasons to love you. Whether you cry or you smile, I love you. When you spill your milk or burp, there is nothing to forgive, there is no fault. You are love, I am love, and we are love."

Today In My World: Be aware of what is going on around you today - truly conscious. Don't make assumptions. Focus on looking behind the obvious.

Week 1 Day 4: Observing The World - It Hurts Just To Listen

Can you absolutely know that it's true?
- Byron Katie

Life only
appears to be
rushing toward us
- jlh

"Oh my God!" we scream as our fragile serenity is overwhelmed by the impending vagaries of LIFE appearing as an unleashed Niagara Falls bearing down upon us.

What if it were only an illusion? Perhaps life is not as threatening as it appears. Perhaps the greatest threat to our serenity is our fear of the future - our fear of the unknown. Perhaps, as Franklin D. Roosevelt said, "The Only Thing We Have to Fear Is Fear Itself."

Stress is to your emotional health as junk food is to your physical health. You need a certain amount of food to sustain your life, but overeating and eating the wrong foods are unhealthy and sometimes dangerous. As you need food to live, you also need a certain amount of emotional stimulation, but unless you choose to live alone far from the reaches of civilization, you are bombarded daily with innumerable stressors (agents, conditions, or other stimuli that cause stress). You hear the daily woes of friends and family. Your job and your daily commute are filled with agitation. Just a few minutes of the 11 o'clock news provides far more than your daily requirement of emotional stimulation. What to do?

1. Simplify your needs: Much of our stress is due to what we believe we need to have. Actually, we need very little - food, a roof over our head, companionship. The rest is all perceived need that causes stress. As a crazy, but everyday example, we get stressed that we don't have the money to finance a relaxing vacation trip. Suppose we just relaxed every day knowing that we don't need luxuries.

2. Simplify your obligations: Practice saying "NO." No, I won't babysit your parakeet. No, I won't work a double shift Sunday. No, I won't chair the fundraising drive. There is actually almost nothing that you must do. Everything in life is a choice. Break the habit of assuming that you need to do everything you are asked to do.

3. Ask yourself what is the worst that can happen: Usually the worst isn't really so bad. For example, the worst your boss can ever do is to fire you, and if you hate your job, that would be a blessing in disguise.

4. Don't be demanding: You ask someone to do something, they don't do it, and you get upset - raising your stress level. Suppose you asked less of other people? Your stress level would go way down. For example, you want your teenagers to keep their rooms tidy. For them, a structured living space is not a priority. Ask yourself whether exerting your control is worth the high stress level that it causes you.

5. Mentally, prepare for failures: Your boss WILL be critical of your work. Your cell phone and computer WILL fail. The stock market WILL drop. There WILL be another terrorist attack or war. It is just life. If you are mentally prepared, you won't be surprised or get stressed when the inevitable happens.

6. Mind your own business: Many of us get upset - and stressed - over the actions of others that are really none of our business. The lifestyle of others is NOT our business. Whether your adult son or daughter has a job, whether they married the "wrong" partner, whether your neighbor recycles, whether the man down the street watches adult movies or his wife is having an affair - these are NOT our business. Know that there is no single way that life is "supposed" to be. Demanding that life meet our expectations is a sure fire recipe for a miserable existence. Life is a game with no rules. Have NO Expectations of life. Stay in your own business and lower your stress.

7. Be grateful for what you have: Each of us has been infinitely blessed - beginning with the gift of life. Whatever may appear to be missing or broken on any particular day, our glass is not half full, it is 99.9% full. More practically, when we feel ungrateful, we become unhappy and stressed. When we choose to feel and express our gratitude, the act of feeling and speaking our thanks creates a happiness within us. The more we express our gratitude, the more we have for which to be grateful.

8. Make YOU your top priority: Your ONLY responsibility in life is to your own happiness. Lower your stress and raise your joy by focusing on yourself. Today and every day, take time to celebrate your life - whether an hour's meditation in a quiet natural space, or a brief moment's conscious pause to breathe deeply and celebrate gratitude for your life.

Today In My World: Throughout your day today, and perhaps in a busy coffee house, be aware of the physical sensations in your body as you listen to various conversations. What kinds of conversations cause a discomfort in your stomach, or a tightening in your shoulders?

Week 1 Day 5: Observing The World - Our Stories

Reality is merely an illusion, albeit a very persistent one.
- Albert Einstein

The eyes are not responsible when the mind does the seeing.
- Publilius Syrus

The world you see has nothing to do with reality. It is of your own making and does not exist.
- A Course In Miracles

Our stories are the window to our emotions.
- jlh

We automatically create a "story" about everything we see or hear or even read.

While "story" is a common word, here we give a special meaning to "story." A "story" is what a person tells themselves has happened or is happening. The story we tell ourselves about a situation is usually different from what a video camera would record. Our story may add to the facts, omit crucial facts, or change facts - either just a little, or completely.

Why do we create stories? Usually we have no idea that we are creating stories. If we have never been exposed to the idea of stories, we may deny that our story about a situation ever differs from the facts. If that is your reaction at this instant, that's OK - let's work from an example.

I have lunch with two friends. Later I find the two arguing about what was said during the lunch. Moreover, I find myself surprised that neither of my friends' recollection of the lunch conversation matches my own.

Each of them has created a "story" to describe the lunch. The "story" is partly based on the events that a video camera would have recorded, but it is also based on each person's history, expectations, emotional state, and much more.

My own recollection of the conversation is also a story!

> *For everything I observe or experience,*
> *I create a story - not sometimes, but always.*
> *- jlh*

Joy is a choice - but not an easy choice. Of course you want to be happy, but life is hard. Your job's a pain, your family nags, and sometimes your body hurts, so how can a Joyful Life be a choice? It isn't an easy choice, but Joy IS a choice that you can make.

Some choices are easy, because clearly defined alternatives are available. Choosing between vanilla and chocolate ice cream is such a choice. Other choices sometimes don't even appear to be choices. If I live in Detroit, but I would prefer to live in Florida, I may not feel that I can choose to relocate. In reality, I always have a choice about where I live. I have my story about how my job, my house, my family, and my friends prevent me from moving, but it is truly only a story.

The greatest obstacle to a Joyful Life is your "story" about your life. Your story is filled with needs and obligations. You are sure that you "need" at least a certain income to live - and you likely feel that you "need" more money than you have. You "need" a "good" job. You "need" a big house. You feel obligated to do whatever your boss and your spouse ask of you. Perhaps you also feel obligated to serve your parents, children, friends, church, and more.

STOP! There is nothing I ever need to have. There is nothing I ever need to do.

> *I say NO to the demands of the world.*
> *I say YES to the longings of my own heart.*
> *- jlh*

The secret to a joyful life is Simplicity - saying NO to the advertisements for the latest this and the most glamorous that - saying NO to chasing that next job promotion - saying NO to all the stressful demands upon your time and energy. It's YOUR time - it's YOUR life - YOU get to choose how you use it.

There is no way that your life is "supposed" to be. Your parents had their vision for your life. Your boss, your spouse, your church, your friends, and even the family next door have their ideas of how you should live your life. What about YOUR vision for your life? What do YOU want? YES, it matters what you want. YES you can have what you want. CHOOSE the life you want, and CHOOSE to live Joyfully.

Today In My World: As you go about your life today, and especially as you observe strangers interacting, consider what story you are creating at each moment.

Week 1 Day 6: Observing The World - Happier Stories

We must let go of the life we have planned, so as to accept the one that is waiting for us.
- Joseph Campbell

Life isn't about finding yourself. Life is about creating yourself.
- George Bernard Shaw

If you wish to see the truth, then hold no opinion for or against.
- Osho

Nothing you believe is true. To know this is freedom.
- Byron Katie

Life is a journey - enjoy the journey. Laugh loudly - laugh often. Laugh at me - laugh at you - laugh at life.
- jlh

Whenever you hear someone telling a story that portrays the speaker as a victim, consider that the person who is being portrayed as a callous villain has their own story to tell. Which story is the right story? That is likely to depend on one's point of view. Neither story is going to be the same as a video camera would have recorded - and perhaps both stories are quite different from the camera version.

Does that mean that a story is wrong to the extent that it doesn't match the video? Not at all. Cameras don't record emotions, and emotions are important. It's just that everyone has their own emotions. What is funny to one person is embarrassing to another.

Imagining alternative stories for everything we see and hear is very powerful, and can protect us from conning ourselves. (Nobody can really con us - we can only do it to ourselves.) Later, we will see that trying-on alternative stories is even more powerful when reviewing our histories, and the painful stories we have made up about our histories.

Today In My World: Throughout today, and especially as you listen to strangers converse, identify your "story" about what you observe, and then "try-on" a happier story for everything you see and hear.

Week 1 Day 7: Observing The World - Go Crazy With Stories

Beware the barrenness of a busy life.
- Socrates

One man's theology is another man's belly laugh.
- Robert A. Heinlein

When you're drowning, you don't say "I would be incredibly pleased if someone would have the foresight to notice me drowning and come and help me," you just SCREAM.
- John Lennon

Time spent laughing is time spent with the gods.
- Japanese Proverb

Life doesn't have to be so serious. It's a lot more fun when we lighten up. Take the nightly news, for example. If we're really going to DO something about the "wrongs" of the world, great - join the Peace Corps or write a big check to Doctors Without Borders. But if all we're going to do by watching the news is upset ourselves, why bother? Most days we would be best off by simply clicking off the news, but today let's try something different.

First, mute the sound. Then pretend the newscaster is wearing a green gorilla suit, just to set the mood, and let his voice be squeaky and fast, like a run away tape recorder. Now let your imagination run wild. Rising oil prices are a conspiracy between the laxative makers of America and the government of Slovonia. The Olympic Torch is fueled with possum tallow, and the protests on TV are the outrage of worldwide possum lovers. The president is actually a space alien in disguise (well, the first two were crazy).

Go wild - have a good chuckle. Whatever you're imagining is no more unreasonable than what the newscaster would usually be saying, and you are actually doing more good for our planet by having a good laugh than you would by just taking the TV stuff until your blood pressure reaches stroke levels.

Today In My World: Get primed by picking up a copy of National ScandalRag at the supermarket checkout and scanning it for some far-out fantasies - like "Elvis sighted wearing mini-dress in Paris", and "Woman gives birth to puppies". Then sit alone in a busy coffee house or another public place. Just observe strangers without interacting with them. Imagine them in crazy costumes that only you can see - talking with squeaky voices. Make up wild stories to explain everything they say. See that threesome at the next table in the green gorilla suits. You know why the short female one is crying? It's because her boyfriend left her for Marilyn Monroe's ghost. Don't stop - keep imagining...

Week 2 Day 1: Observing Family and Friends - Belonging

To err is human; to forgive, divine.
- Alexander Pope

It is a good thing to learn caution from the misfortunes of others.
- Publilius Syrus

One of the oldest human needs is having someone to wonder where you are when you don't come home at night.
- Margaret Mead

Love them as they are, and forgive them everything.
- jlh

This week, we're going to do almost the same thing as last week, but it will feel completely different. We have a history with family and friends, and that history drives EVERYTHING we think we see and hear our family and friends do and say. Our "story" about EVERYTHING they do and say is so strong that there is hardly even a resemblance between one of our "stories" and the video camera version.

For this whole week, we will focus on observing our friends and family interact with each other. Last week, we focused on interactions between people we did not know personally, and in a later week we will finally focus on observing our own interactions with other people. This is a very important sequence that is crucial to the success of our seven week program. We are the most detached from and objective about the speaking and actions of those we do not know personally, and the most intertwined with - and therefore the least objective about - our own interactions. The interactions of our friends and family with each other occur at a midpoint in our ability to be objective.

Today In My World: Today, notice everything your friends and family do or say that doesn't appear to be in their best interest. Do they gossip? complain? How do they look - attentive? eye contact? preoccupied? How do they sound - stressed? or calm? afraid? angry?

What are your body sensations when your friends and family are unkind to each other, or when they do not do or say what you wish they would? Do your stomach and shoulders feel different when you watch friends or family argue than when you observe strangers bickering?

When you observe friends and family behaving differently than you would want, are you angry? resentful? embarrassed?

Week 2 Day 2: Observing Family and Friends - Approval

If I had a prayer, it would be this: "God spare me from the desire for love, approval, or appreciation." Amen.
 - Byron Katie

Keep away from people who try to belittle your ambitions. Small people always do that, but the really great make you feel that you, too, can become great.
- Mark Twain

The world is unfathomable. And so are we, and so is every being that exists in this world.
- Carlos Castaneda

We all want other people to like us and approve of us. That approval can take many forms. It isn't always as obvious as the "A" on the term paper or the salary increase from our boss. A woman may seek Valentine's Day flowers, a Mother's day dinner, or a gift of jewelry as tangible forms of approval. For a man, sex is one principal form of approval - "if you approve of me as a virile handsome man, you will want to show me your approval by having sex with me." Another form of approval-seeking is to model ourselves on people we admire.

You do not need anyone's permission to be your true self
- jlh

Today In My World: Today, notice everything your friends and family say and do that demonstrates their need for approval and recognition. Sometimes it is obvious, such as "you don't love me anymore." Other times it is more subtle: "It's been a while since we've been to lunch together." Consider that a statement such as, "I was on my feet a lot today." is also a cry for approval.

How do you feel when you identify a cry for approval in something someone close to you says or does?

Week 2 Day 3: Observing Family and Friends - Judgments

You can't be compassionate when you're sitting in judgment.
 - Sheri Rosenthal

Peace of mind comes from not wanting to change others.
 - Gerald Jampolsky

Would you prefer that you be right or happy?
 - A Course In Miracles

I have no need to conform to the stereotypes others have defined for me.
 - jlh

Whenever you hear anyone use a phrase like "you should," "you shouldn't," "you must," "you ought to," or "you can't," someone is minding someone else's business. We all use those words, and we all meddle in each other's business. We can't completely stop it, but we can be conscious and attempt to limit our meddling.

Here are five questions to ask yourself before offering helpful advice...

1. Did the other person ask for help, advice, or opinion? If the answer is No, then I am meddling. The first and greatest rule is, Unsolicited Advice Is Always Meddling

2. Even if the person has broadcast a request for help or advice, did they ask for MY advice? When someone is drowning, they will accept a life-ring thrown by a stranger, but advice is only appreciated if the asker fully trusts and respects the advisor.

3. Do I fully respect the other person? While I can responsibly make decisions for a child or a senile person, it is pure meddling for me to believe that I know better than another competent adult how they should live their life. As an example, trying to find friends for someone who has clearly expressed a preference for solitude is meddling.

4. Is the issue a question of belief? Proselytizing is always meddling. My beliefs about religion, politics, the best natural supplements, or whatever, are just my personal beliefs, nothing more. If someone ASKS, I am happy to share about what gives my own life joy and meaning, but whenever I attempt to convert someone else's beliefs, I must be very clear that I am doing it for my own gains, and not as a service to the other.

5. Have I previously attempted to assist this person with this same issue in the past? If I have been asked again, and if I find a different way to be helpful, it's not meddling, but if I continually offer the same advice for the same problem, it crosses

the line into meddling. Compassion and generosity may well be the greatest human virtues, but it is also important to avoid letting these noble instincts cause inadvertent harm to those we want to help.

Today In My World: Become aware of all the times you hear someone make a "suggestion" or otherwise attempt to alter the behaviors of others.

How do you feel when you observe these subtle, and not so subtle, attempts to control others?

Week 2 Day 4: Observing Family and Friends - Open Heart

There is no truth, only human opinion.
- Anonymous

Everyone is a prisoner of his own experiences.
No one can eliminate prejudices - just recognize them.
- Edward R. Murrow

Because we believe that our ethnic group, our society, our political party, our God, is better than your God, we kill each other.
- Neale Donald Walsch

Few people are capable of expressing with equanimity opinions which differ from the prejudices of their social environment. Most people are even incapable of forming such opinions.
- Albert Einstein

It is a truism that almost any sect, cult, or religion will legislate its creed into law if it acquires the political power to do so.
- Robert A. Heinlein

Every form of addiction is bad, no matter whether the narcotic be alcohol or morphine or idealism.
- Carl Jung

Universal compassion is the only guarantee of morality.
- Arthur Schopenhauer

The golden rule is that there are no golden rules.
- George Bernard Shaw

EVERYONE believes that their BELIEFS are the RIGHT ones; that's why they're called "beliefs."
- jlh

Respect Your Mind. Faith is powerful, but it is no substitute for observing, paying attention, weighing alternatives, and choosing with intention. Without conscious choice, there is no freedom or happiness.

> *It ain't what you don't know that gets you into trouble.*
> *It's what you know for sure that just ain't so.*
> *- Mark Twain*

If you know it "for sure," it probably isn't truth to everyone else. We are most sure about those things to which we have given the least thought. If you KNOW that something is true without having ever questioned it, take the opportunity to consider the opinions of others with an open mind.

Joy blooms where minds and hearts are open.
- jlh

Open your mind to new thoughts. Pack your ancient and honored traditions respectfully, and store them in the attic of your past, to remember on days of reminiscence. Open your heart to diversity. Love everyone without prejudice or bias. Honor the trainings of your youth by choosing to reinforce the lessons of universal love, while discarding the lessons of fear and exclusion. Love and honor yourself, those with whom you feel close, those who challenge you, and those you have yet to meet. Make it a conscious daily practice to love and honor yourself and all others.

Today In My World: Today, look for examples of prejudice in action, and examples of bias being used in hurtful ways. Do you like or dislike what is said? Do you think something different "should" have been said? Do you feel the desire to add your own opinion to the conversation of others?

Week 2 Day 5: Observing Family and Friends - Life Is A Mirror

I had forgotten how much light there is in the world, 'til you gave it back to me.
- Ursula Le Guin

Simply put, you believe that things or people make you unhappy, but this is not accurate. You make yourself unhappy.
 - Wayne Dyer

Everyone is a mirror image of yourself - your own thinking coming back at you.
- Byron Katie

What others say and do is a projection of their own reality.
 - don Miguel Ruiz

Everything that irritates us about others can lead us to an understanding of ourselves.
 - Carl Jung

We see Life through the fun-house mirrors of our point-of-view.
- jlh

Life is a mirror and will reflect back to the thinker what he thinks into it.
- Ernest Holmes

I would paraphrase Dr. Holmes quote as "Life is a mirror and reflects my intent back to me." This has a dual meaning: First - if I feel angry with a person, I will see that person as being an angry person. Second - and the flip side of the same coin - if I see a person as being an angry person, I can be certain that I have been directing my own anger toward that person. We call this tendency to attribute our own emotions to those around us *projection*.

We never see Life as it really is. All we can ever see is the reflection of Life - distorted by our unique perceptions.

We tend see what we are expecting to see. Sometimes we expect to see want we want to see. Other times, we see what we fear. Either way, we are usually neither alert nor objective.

May your mind whirl joyful cartwheels of creativity.
May your heart sing sweet lullabies of timelessness.
May your essence be the nectar of the open blossom of your joy.
May your spirit soar throughout the vast cathedral of your being.
- jlh

Life is magnificent - just as it comes. Our life is the greatest gift of all creation. When we are unhappy with life - when we are shocked by the stock market, or dismayed by our choice of political candidates, let's not lash out in anger. But also, let's not try to pretty up life with some lipstick and some party clothes. See life clearly - no rose colored glasses - and then CHOOSE to love life. CHOOSE to be happy, be joyful, be grateful, be forgiving of everyone and of every act we believe has hurt us. Life just "IS." We get to CHOOSE our relationship with life.

Life is all in the perspective we take on it.
- jlh

Today is a day to look at our life from different and broader perspectives. As we watch the stock market plummet, real estate values continue to decline, and our employment future in question, today would be a good day to look at our lives from a perspective of thankfulness for what we have and a perspective of wonder at our very existence and the magnificence of the world we live in.

Unexpected events can set you back or set you up.
It's all a matter of - perspective.
- Mary Anne Radmacher

Life can look different from a distance: Put some distance between yourself and whatever is concerning you. Distance in space or time always creates a new perspective.

Get up-close-and-personal: Life looks different when you really get involved.

Look at Life in a Different Light: Shine a bright light on your issues, or turn off the spotlight and take a broader view.

Look from a Different Angle: Approach life from a new angle. Assume nothing.

Pretend You Just Got to America: We just don't see what is familiar. When we go to a foreign land we really SEE because we don't already ASSUME what will be there. Pretend your community is a foreign land and really SEE it. SEE your blessings.

See Life as Play: Who said that life has to be serious?

See How Blessed We Are: We have more comfort, more wealth, and better health than ever before in history or anywhere else in the world. If we are not happy, perhaps we should count our blessings.

Choose to See Beauty and Joy: Much in life can be seen as ugly or beautiful - it's our choice. Why would we choose to see any part of life as ugly?

Choose to Celebrate Life: Choose to view life from the perspective of Celebration. Celebrate family, celebrate friends, celebrate love, celebrate different perspectives, celebrate and give thanks for all of life.

Today In My World: As you overhear conversations today, watch for examples of the miscommunication that occurs when the listener attributes motives to the speaker that are unrelated to the context of the conversation. How do you feel when you hear this occurring?

Week 2 Day 6: Observing Family and Friends - Perspective

There are no right answers to wrong questions.
- Ursula LeGuin

The Tao abides in non-action, Yet nothing is left undone.
- Lao Tzu (Tao Te Ching)

The Master acts without doing, and everything gets done.
- (alternate translation of the previous Tao Te Ching passage)

The intuitive mind is a sacred gift and the rational mind is a faithful servant. We have created a society that honors the servant and has forgotten the gift.
- Albert Einstein

Well, you ask a silly question, and you get a silly answer.
- Tom Lehrer

Happiness is a function of accepting what is.
- Werner Erhard

When I let go of what I am, I become what I might be.
- Lao Tzu

Feeling important makes one heavy, clumsy and vain. To be a warrior one needs to be light and fluid.
- Carlos Castaneda

It would be insane for me to lose sleep over your opinions.
- jlh

Caring about someone is not an excuse to try to live their life for them. If you choose to be helpful, help others to achieve the life THEY desire, not the life you wish for them.

The #1 Secret of Great Relationships...

Behind all the issues that separate an ordinary relationship from a great one, is one common factor. Behind all the truly helpful advice on improving your life together, there lies one key to a great relationship.

Many different kinds of problems can cause a relationship to fall apart. Physical or emotional abuse, addictions, cheating, jealousy, and neediness are just a few of the issues that can destroy a relationship. But once the many potentially disastrous problems have been avoided, what have you got? Perhaps a relationship that qualifies only as "pretty good." But what creates a really great relationship?

At the beginning, we are in relationship because we are attracted to the other person - we think they are sexy, smart, funny, whatever it is that we find appealing. But very quickly, the focus of the relationship turns to whether we feel appreciated. If we don't feel appreciated, we don't feel loved.

It is common for those entering into a relationship to hold an idealized image of how a perfect partner is supposed to act. Perhaps a man is supposed to open car doors. Perhaps a woman is supposed to wear a certain kind of underwear. The internal dialog goes something like this, "Jim (or Sally) is a wonderful person and loves me. After we're together, he will change because he loves me so much. He will stop wanting to hang out with his friends, watch football games, whatever." How can anyone feel appreciated when their loved one is wishing or hoping for them to change.

The greatest roadblock to a great relationship is trying to force a partner to change through bribes or threats. This classic human tendency is lampooned in the long-running off-Broadway musical comedy "I Love You, You're Perfect, Now Change." It's funny to watch other people go through the cycle of searching for the perfect mate, believing they have found that person, and than gradually attempting to remold the supposedly perfect partner. Unfortunately, in real life, this pattern is a cause of immense suffering.

I Love You Just the Way You Are

The number one secret of a great relationship is accepting our partner EXACTLY as they are. We cause ourselves untold misery whenever we believe our loved ones to be imperfect and try to change them.

To create a great relationship, say and mean, "I love you just the way you are." No pretense. No hoping for change. No thought that it used to be better, or might get better. Follow through by living into that sentiment every day.

Falling into the trap of thinking, "I wish you were different" or "Please change." is no way to show your love. Happiness lies in this number one rule of great relationships: Love and accept your partner exactly the way they are.

Today In My World: Observe how often you are tempted to meddle in someone else's business. You are meddling whenever you believe that you are the best judge of how a another person should live their life, what they should believe, or what they should want.

Week 2 Day 7: Observing Family and Friends - Dance Lightly

Life is without meaning. You bring the meaning to it. The meaning of life is whatever you ascribe it to be. Being alive is the meaning.
- Joseph Campbell

The more I see, the less I know for sure.
- John Lennon

The more you see, the less you know.
- Bono (City Of Blinding Lights)

Don't let one cloud obliterate the whole sky.
- Anais Nin

A tree that is unbending is easily broken.
- Lao Tzu

God has no religion.
- Mohandas Gandhi

The world is incomprehensible. We won't ever understand it. Thus we must treat the world as it is: a sheer mystery.
- Carlos Castaneda

Become "a lover of what is."
- Byron Katie

Nature does not hurry, yet everything is accomplished.
- Lao Tzu

Hurrying - urgency - robs life of its quality. Patience is more than a virtue, patience is a joyful way of living. Don't accomplish less, but focus on the most important things, and proceed at a natural comfortable pace. The soft water of the river cuts through the hardest rock - in its own time.

The River of Life has no meaning - no good, no bad,
no better, no worse, no love, no hate, no fear, no anger, no joy.
The River of Life has no judgment, no expectation.
The River of Life just IS.
- jlh

The River of Life meanders without apparent purpose. To question Life is to invite suffering. To attempt to overpower Life is to tilt at windmills. Life is best enjoyed without resistance. Surrender to the flow of the River of Life, yet do not float down the river like a leaf or a log. While neither attempting to resist time nor to to hurry it, become the rudder and use your energy to correct your course to avoid the whirlpools and undertow.

Most unhappiness comes from resisting life. Occasionally, we have such a strong commitment to changing the world order that it is worth struggling against the flow of life. Perhaps you have a cause such as universal veganism - your life is committed to preventing even one more animal from being eaten by anyone. But most people don't have that kind of dedication to a cause, and even for those who do, there is much of daily life that is not related to any particular issue of principle.

Nonetheless, we live our lives as if each minor happening were a matter of life and death. Our favorite restaurant has run out of today's blackboard special. The bananas in the grocery store are all green. The drawbridge is stuck in the "up" position. We have demands of the world, these demands aren't met, and we become disappointed and angry. Is that just human nature? Yes and no. It is human nature to prefer the predictable, but this preference becomes highly exaggerated in some societies.

Twenty First Century America, especially in dense urban areas, has become the epitome of expectations and demands, which inevitably result in disappointment and anger as the world fails to meet these expectations. Demanding that the world meet our expectations has become a bad habit that causes great unhappiness. But it doesn't have to be that way.

We can break the bad habit of being unhappy. Think of life being like a mighty river, such as the Mississippi or the Amazon. Sometimes the river floods, sometimes it quiets. Sometimes it cuts a new course, drowning some farmland and leaving some old river bottom high and dry. One could fight the river and curse its vicissitudes, or one could sail on the river, fish in the river, drink from the river, irrigate crops from the river, and live happily on the river.

Fighting against life, like fighting against a mighty river is a pointless waste of energy and upset. Within the constraints life sets and within its vagaries, we still have immense freedom of action. We can fully express our commitments and live life to the fullest without fighting against it.

To go with the flow of life, without compromising your values:

1. Visualize life as a river, and the challenge of living as being a river pilot. Keep your eye far enough downstream that you can gently maneuver toward your goal using the force of the river to power your journey. Think of setting your course as the game that it is. Outthink life, but don't try to overpower it.

2. Remember that life is not serious. You already know the final score: Life-1, You-0. So just have fun on your run down the river.

3. Take time for yourself. Breathe deeply. Take a quiet walk. Spend time alone in a natural setting and soak up the stillness.

4. Clear your mind of everything you thought you knew. Be like a child in having no preconceptions of how life should turn out. Visualize pouring water into a cup. That's like life flowing into a young child. Now visualize trying to pour clear water into a cup filled with mud. That is like the flow of creation being resisted by expectations and demands one attempts to place upon life.

5. Be grateful for all of life. Be thankful you are alive. Not to be thankful for life is to be like a starving person who is gifted a steak and complains that it is tough.

6. Dance lightly with life. Dancing with life is like dancing with an elephant. She makes a jolly partner so long as you watch her moves, react quickly, and don't get stepped on.

Today In My World: Today, like The River of Life, go with the flow. Whenever you observe yourself making a value judgment about anything, consider the possibility that nothing is really wrong, and that the world is really doing just fine exactly as it is.

Week 3 Day 1: Observing Myself - Silence and Solitude

There are only two ways to live your life. One is as though nothing is a miracle. The other is as though everything is a miracle.
- Albert Einstein

In silence you hear who you are becoming. You create yourself.
- Jewel

I am a unique expression of the universal fabric of creation.
- jlh

My father considered a walk among the mountains as the equivalent of churchgoing.
- Aldous Huxley

I often regret that I have spoken; never that I have been silent.
- Publilius Syrus

Donkey, you HAVE the right to remain silent. What you lack, is the capacity.
- said by Shrek in the movie Shrek 2

Few people know how to take a walk. The qualifications are endurance, plain clothes, old shoes, an eye for nature, good humor, vast curiosity, good speech, good silence and nothing too much.
- Ralph Waldo Emerson

Angels whisper to a man when he goes for a walk.
- Raymond Inmon

In every walk with nature one receives far more than he seeks.
- John Muir

Nothing is missing - it's all an illusion.
- jlh

In this third week of our program, having observed strangers, friends, and family, we finally move our focus onto ourselves. In a sense, each of us is absolutely unique, but at the same time, we all share the same basic elements of being human. Almost all the habits and behaviors that you observed in others over the last two weeks are also your own burdens, at least to some degree.

I don't know the key to success,
but the key to failure is to try to please everyone.
- Bill Cosby

Sometimes the pressure to please our spouse, our boss, our family and friends, our church, our community can seem overwhelming. Take William Shakespeare's advise, "*To thine own self be true*." Your life and your choices are yours alone.

Happiness is not something anyone else can give us... or take away from us. Happiness is what we make of our lives... or don't. Whatever our circumstances, we can create a joyful life... or a miserable life. It is up to us. Here are seven secrets for a happy life...

1. Respect Yourself: If I don't love and respect myself, who will? It all starts right here with ME. If I think that I'm a pretty good person, it doesn't much matter what anyone else thinks. And the irony is that once I like myself, most everyone else will like me too. People enjoy being around people who speak well of themselves - not in an arrogant boastful way, but with honest self-appreciation.

2. Forgive Everyone for Everything: Angry and happy don't mix. Flush out the angry, and the happy has a place to put down roots. Until we forgive everyone for everything, we hold on to anger and resentment. Once we forgive, we can become happy. Forgiving is not a gift to someone else - Forgiving is our gift to ourselves - a great gift - the gift of happiness.

3. Be Grateful for All of Life: Each of us has been infinitely blessed - beginning with the gift of life. Whatever may appear to be missing or broken on any particular day, our glass is not half full, it is 99.9% full. More practically, when we feel ungrateful, we become unhappy. When we choose to feel and express our gratitude, the act of feeling and speaking our thanks creates a happiness within us. The more we express our gratitude, the more we have for which to be grateful. Today and every day, take time to celebrate life - whether an hour's meditation in a quiet natural space, or a brief moment's conscious pause to breathe deeply and celebrate gratitude for life.

4. Choose Happiness: Everything in life is a choice. There is never anything we ever "need" to do. Every action and thought is a choice and has consequences - pleasant or unpleasant. Whether you go to work today, change jobs, smile at the bank teller, yell at your kids, complain about life, hold a daily celebration of gratitude for life - they are all choices. Happiness is a choice. Stay alert and make conscious choices for happiness.

5. Begin at the End: You can never reach your destination if you don't have a destination. Decide what accomplishments you want recorded on your tombstone. Take a whole quiet day to consider your life. Be very clear that your happiness does NOT depend on reaching your goal. In fact, it's the reverse. Your happiness depends on accepting whatever life throws at you while you walk the path toward your goal. What is important for your happiness is having a goal, and working toward it.

6. Start Today: Whatever you want in life, start today. Not tomorrow - today. Let it be a small beginning - a tiny beginning. Your happiness depends on starting today - every day.

7. Accept that Life is NOT "Supposed to be Fair": Know that there is no single way that life is "supposed" to be. Demanding that life meet our expectations is a sure fire recipe for a miserable existence. Life is a game with no rules. Life just happens to us regardless of our best intentions. Our only path to happiness lies in being open to receiving whatever life throws at us - with Gratitude. Have NO Expectations of life.

The following exercise is from *Simply an Inspired Life: Consciously Choosing Unbounded Happiness in Good Times & Bad* by Jonathan Lockwood Huie and Mary Anne Radmacher, courtesy of Conari Press.

Today In My World: Tomorrow morning, get up 1/2 hour early, and go for a walk around the neighborhood - alone, and in complete silence - leaving your iPod and cell phone at home. For the first half of your walk, just pay attention to your surroundings, and observe your thoughts (stories) about the things you see on your walk.

On the second half of your walk, TRY to keep your mind blank - no thinking - no stories - no explanations for ANYTHING.

When your let your thoughts roll, what stories did you create? What irritated you, and what stories did you create about why it irritated you? Were you able to stop the stories when you tried? Probably not. The nature of being human is to create non-stop stories.

Week 3 Day 2: Observing Myself - I Am the Wizard

All you have to do is look straight and see the road, and when you see it, don't sit looking at it - walk.
- Ayn Rand

Can you let go of words and ideas, attitudes and expectations? If so, then the Tao will loom into view.
- Lao Tzu

Those who are highly evolved maintain an undiscriminating perception. Seeing everything, labeling nothing, they maintain their awareness of the Great Oneness. Thus they are supported by it.
- Lao Tzu

The power of the Wizard lives within me. I call upon its magic at will - transforming Fear into Love.
- jlh

To the young child, all life is a great adventure - when did we grow so dull and brittle.
- jlh

I Am the Wizard
I am the Wizard. This world is mine.
I speak. It's done. My realm is fine.
My wand, my tongue. My sword, my voice.
It's good. It's bad. I speak my choice.
I say happy, or I say mad.
I say angry, or I say glad.
I name that drawing on the wall.
It's not graffiti after all.
The past has been broken. The prison's not real.
My word holds the magic - the power to heal.
Intent is my weapon - a sword from above.
Cruel hate, fear, and anger transmute into love.
This world's my joy. This mouth's my toy.
Reborn -I'm a brand new girl or boy.
I choose. I speak. My will is done.
Come join. Come play. This can be fun.
- jlh

Your power is unlimited, whether you call the force you access intention or call it prayer. Perhaps today is a day to be lighthearted and visualize fairy dust or a wizard's wand as you perform your magic - transforming suffering into happiness.

We attract abundance when we ask from a compassionate heart.
- jlh

There is no scientific basis whatsoever for the "Law of Attraction," as there is no scientific basis for anything else in metaphysics or in religion. Does that mean all of metaphysics is wrong? No, just un-provable.

Is intent - or intention - real? While not scientifically provable, intent is certainly very real in my personal experience, and the experience of many I know well.

My Intent is my transmission to the entire Universe. It is the way I speak my vision for the future. While I can "speak" anything to the Universe, many transmissions are not received or are diverted.

My compassionate intents are generally received clearly and acted upon - perhaps not immediately, or in exactly the way I hope- but acted upon favorably, nonetheless.

However desires that are neutral - such as my desire to win the lottery - are just ignored. Further, my harmful or "evil" desires are not only rejected by the Universe, but are mirrored back to me as intense personal suffering - essentially Hell-on-earth.

The usual expression of the "Law of Attraction" states that the Universe will give you ANYTHING you want. That is half-true in that you can have anything that you request with compassion. The untruth is the expectation that the Universe will respond favorably when you ask for money or ask to harm others.

Consider the distinction between affluence and riches. Affluence is a state of mind. I can perceive affluence regardless of my external circumstances. The Universe responds favorably when I request affluence. I always receive the feeling of having everything I need. Sometimes I actually receive riches, and sometimes I receive that satisfied feeling with what the Universe deems is best for me. Either way, I truly receive affluence.

If you prefer to use the phrase "Law of Attraction," just remember that it will provide what you request with compassion, but not satisfy your hurtful or greedy requests.

Today In My World: Take another silent early morning walk. Today invent a nonsense name for everything you notice. That old soda bottle in the street is a "fuft" - the marks on that wall are "scribs". When your monkey mind starts to tell you a story about what you see, thank your mind and return to inventing nonsense names. Does your body feel different than yesterday?

Week 3 Day 3: Observing Myself - I Choose My World

I hope that you walk around the corner and you get very surprised.
- Miranda Richardson

Life is like a sewer... what you get out of it depends on what you put into it.
- Tom Lehrer

There are very few human beings who receive the complete truth by instant illumination. Most of us acquire it fragment by small fragment.
- Anis Nin (paraphrase jlh)

Yesterday is ashes; tomorrow green wood. Only today does the fire burn brightly.
- Eskimo proverb

Spirit is always waiting to rush into us, but we are too full of worldly things. It is like trying to pour fine wine into a cup filled with mud - the wine is waiting, but the mud must be removed first.
- jlh

I say "YES" to the opportunities life offers me.
- jlh

The beauty does not live out there; the beauty's in my eyes.
- jlh

Today Is A Beautiful Day
Today is crisp and cool yet warm; the sky glows dull yet bright.
It rains, it's dry, it's clear, it clouds; it always feels just right.
The city streets, the woodsy path; they're all the same to me.
That pile of trash, that bloom of rose; both beauty fine to see.
The tears, the smiles, the pain, the ease; today is what I've got.
I change not fact, but what I see, with Joy I cast my lot.
The beauty does not live out there; the beauty's in my eyes.
The scene may change, the cast may leave; the beauty never dies.
- jlh

External circumstances are mostly beyond our control, but we can always choose our outlook on life. In that sense, you are in complete control of your life. You choose the world you will live in - a world of suffering, or a world of joy.

Here are Nine Secrets for Getting Un-Stuck and Taking Charge of Your Life...

1. Believe in yourself. A daily affirmation may seem to be a silly idea, but give it a try anyway. Write your own affirmation about your abilities, and repeat it each day before you leave your home. Start with the following, and modify it until it fully expresses your commitments, beliefs, and intents.

I am unlimited. I take responsibility for my life.
My every action is a conscious choice.
I can accomplish anything good that I truly set my mind on.
I keep focus, and persevere.

2. Make peace with your past. In the words of William Shakespeare, "What's done is done." You can't change the past. You can't undo any actions you took or failed to take. Your only choice today is either to waste energy and emotion on regrets and resentments, or to treat your own past like a history book - an interesting, but emotionally neutral, recitation of ancient times.

3. See each day as a new beginning. Don't project your past onto your future. Suppose you won the lottery yesterday, would that mean you will win the lottery again tomorrow? Usually, we are fairly realistic about not expecting a run of good fortune to continue, but when we hit a streak of bad luck, we tend to project that failure into our future and think times will never get better. So you stepped on a banana peel and slipped yesterday, does that mean it will happen again tomorrow? If you got fired or your lover left, it's unfortunate, but there's always tomorrow - a tomorrow that can shine so long as you don't project yesterday's shadow upon it.

4. Look for the best in people. Everyone has good points and bad. Everyone will please you at times and annoy you at others. While there is power in choosing to associate mostly with positive people, there is even more power in seeing the best in everyone. Everyone has a lesson to teach us. Let the impact of an unkind or thoughtless word last only a moment, but bask for a whole day in gentle words and insightful thoughts. The happiest among us have no enemies.

5. Make a gratitude list, and review it often. Not everything has gone well in your life, but much has. Too often we focus on the negative and forget our great blessings - health, friends, family, beauty, nature, our body, our mind, Spirit, life itself. Perhaps you have arthritis or your spouse just moved out. Yes, those are big negatives, but your list, anyone's list, of blessings is vastly larger than any list of problems.

6. Design your future. Visualize being in the future you desire. Make that vision so real you can taste and smell it - a three-dimensional full-color motion picture with surround-sound. That is your goal - your destination. Never forget it - never lose track of it. Let what you do every day be done with that vision in mind. Be the aspiring athlete or musician whose every day moves them one inch closer to that three-minute mile or perfect concerto.

7. Either learn how to enjoy your work, or get a new career. Make a list of what you like and what you dislike about your job. Perhaps you enjoy your customers and co-workers, but find your boss annoying. Limit your awareness of the annoying times to the moment in which they occur, but let thoughts of the service and camaraderie permeate your day. If you find that the frustrations of your job outweigh the enjoyment, get a new career. Whatever your interests, there is a way to do something you enjoy, make a difference in the world, and get well paid at the same time. Make a list of all your interests and abilities, and think big. Don't let anyone else's small and limited thinking deter you from your goal.

8. Enjoy everything you do, or don't do it. Yes, you have to file your taxes and stop at stop signs whether you like it or not. This secret refers to those things you do merely out of habit or to avoid embarrassment. Enjoy that party, or don't accept the invitation. Feel fulfilled by that volunteer committee, or don't join. Believe in that particular charitable cause, or don't contribute. Everything in life is a choice - make wise choices that maximize your happiness.

9. Feel Unity with Spirit and all creation. You are never alone. Your Higher Power, whatever that means to you, is a constant support - never hesitate to ask for guidance and blessing. Remember that Spirit knows better than you what is best for you, so ask for comfort and affluence rather than the affections of a particular person or a higher paying job. Whatever your circumstances, and however often you may have felt rejected, there are many people in this world who live in the tradition of the "Good Samaritan." When troubles weigh upon you, do not hesitate to find and rely upon these people - they are far more numerous than you think.

Exercise: For the next 60 seconds, EVERYTHING is right with my world - because I say it is!

Today In My World: Take another walk in silence. On today's walk, give everything a favorable name. That's not trash, it's decorations. Not graffiti, but wall art. Not storm clouds, but spring flowers being delivered. How are your body sensations today?

Week 3 Day 4: Observing Myself - Up Is Down & Down Is Up

The way I see it, it doesn't matter what you believe, just so you're sincere.
- Linus Van Pelt in Charles M. Schulz' Go Fly A Kite, Charlie Brown

To you I'm an atheist; to God, I'm the Loyal Opposition.
- the Woody Allen movie Stardust Memories

A foolish consistency is the hobgoblin of little minds.
  - Ralph Waldo Emerson

I make it a policy to try never to make a complete idiot of myself twice in the same way. After all, there's always all kinds of new ways to make a complete idiot of myself. Why repeat the old ones?
- Margot Dalton

Anyone who has never made a mistake has never tried anything new.
- Albert Einstein

The world is perfect the way it is.
- Werner Erhard

There's no wrong, only discovery...
  - Byron Katie

There is no "right", there is no "wrong" - there are just points of view.
- jlh

The Paradox Of Living In The Moment - How To Be Happy Today And Prepare For Tomorrow

Are you feeling stressed and upset? If so, you are worrying about tomorrow. Events that have already occurred may cause you regret, but they only appear to cause worry. If you just lost your job, you are not worrying about losing your job - that already happened. You are worrying about paying your bills and finding a new job. Those are worries about tomorrow.

Worrying is just a natural human emotion, and everyone worries, right? Actually not. Worry is a bad habit that most people acquire, and like all habits, can be broken.

When you worry about what may or may not occur in the future, you miss the joy that is available today - each and every day. So is the answer to focus only on today, and let tomorrow take care of itself? That sounds good - until tomorrow arrives and you are not prepared.

It's a paradox. How does one balance living in the now with preparing responsibly for the future? The key to this dilemma lies in the distinction between "worrying about the future," and "preparing for the future."

The two concepts are not at all the same. There are two aspects to preparing for the future. The one that is more familiar to most people is planning. You know the mortgage is due next week so you save the money - You know you want to fit into your clothes tomorrow, so you forgo that second helping. Planning for the future is fully compatible with living joyfully today.

The other aspect of preparing for the future is accepting that things will probably not turn out the way you plan. Creating this acceptance of life's uncertainties is much more challenging than formulating and following through on plans.

The source of most worry is a lack of acceptance of the uncertainties of the future. When one fully lives a life of acceptance, life's vagaries are not merely tolerated, but are enjoyed because they are life's gifts. If one is religiously inclined, whatever life delivers is a gift from the Creator. If one holds other beliefs, then whatever happens is just what there is to work with - so why not enjoy it.

The recipe for a joyful life is planning and preparing for the future, while simultaneously accepting that you hold virtually no control over future events. By placing no demands on the future, you can enjoy whatever it brings.

We live in a crazy world. We will never understand the mind of God. What is the intent of the divine? Or is life random chance?

An exercise that holds great power is temporarily adopting actions or beliefs that are opposite to our usual behaviors and convictions. examples would be a usually flashy dresser going into the day in sweat pants or a shy person telling jokes.

Today In My World: While you walk alone in silence today, either get religion or give it up. Just for this 30 minute walk, pretend that everything happens by random chance (or is guided by the hand of God - whichever concept is unfamiliar and uncomfortable). What is your experience of today's walk? What are your thoughts? How are your body sensations today?

Week 3 Day 5: Observing Myself - My Hate Hurts Me Most

If you judge people, you have no time to love them.
- Mother Teresa

I'm sure we all agree that we ought to love one another and I know there are people in the world that do not love their fellow human beings and I HATE people like that.
- Tom Lehrer

Don't be against anything - e.g. don't be against war, be FOR peace.
- jlh

God is equally available to all people.
- jlh

Hate, anger, and especially the instinct toward vengeance cause great suffering. Here are three major reasons to purge all thoughts and feelings of vengeance from your life:

1. It is abhorrent to value systems that honor compassion.

2. Lusting after vengeance raises your blood pressure, makes you physically and emotionally unhealthy, and causes your life to be dominated by suffering rather than joy.

3. It doesn't work. Whether personal or international, vengeance begets more vengeance in an unending cycle.

The Buddha says, "*Hate is never conquered by hate, Hate is only conquered by love.*"

Jesus says, "*You have heard that it was said, 'Eye for eye, and tooth for tooth.' But I tell you, Do not resist an evil person. If someone strikes you on the right cheek, turn to him the other also. You have heard that it was said, 'Love your neighbor and hate your enemy.' But I tell you: Love your enemies and pray for those who persecute you.*" (Matthew 5:38-39,43-44)

Ever heard of the Hatfield-McCoy feud? In the post-Civil War period, these families indulged in reciprocal murder in the hills of West Virginia and Kentucky. In several ways, the feud was typical of feuds throughout history. It began in a small way and escalated. Belief systems were involved (the families had been on opposite sides of the Civil War). Honor, land, and tangible property were at stake. Some say it began as an argument over a pig. One way in which it was not typical is that it was over in thirty years. Some of the world's great feuds have been fought continuously for over a thousand years.

The Hatfield-McCoy feud is a useful example because few if any people alive today have a vested interest in it. It is relatively easy to see that killing each other over a pig, small amounts of money, accusations of lying, a clandestine affair, and the like, is sheer foolishness. But what about the feuds in which we are personally involved - both interpersonal and international.

My first instinct whenever I have been injured is to seek revenge. I believe it's a human reaction that is as old as humanity itself. A business partner didn't repay a large loan to me. I wanted revenge. I was sued over something that wasn't my fault. I wanted revenge. Clearly the act of wanting revenge is counterproductive. Anger and hate are unpleasant emotions. In my quest to live a joyful life, anger and hate have no place.

But suppose I could succeed in my vengeance? Wouldn't I feel really good? Maybe briefly, but the elation would be short-lived. Achieving victory at the expense of someone else's suffering isn't my cup of tea. Moreover, the vengeance would escalate, because no one wants to feel a perceived dishonor. Since I have made the choice to stop my anger, hate, and vengeance, my life has been far happier and healthier.

Vengeance on an international scale is just a larger version of the Hatfield-McCoy feud. Anger, hatred, murder, revenge killing. Generation after generation murdering in an attempt to extract vengeance for the deeds of their ancestors. Where does it stop? Sometimes one side prevails militarily for a time. Then what? Perhaps the defeated party gains renewed strength and resumes the battle. If the weaker side remains subjugated, they develop the attitude and skills of a cornered ferret. They will fight to the death - house to house - as in Palestine today.

Do feuds ever end? Only when both sides shake hands, and agree that there is no winner, no loser, only people who have wearied of fighting and desire to live in peace. For many years, Northern Ireland was locked in a murderous and seemingly unending feud. The key to ending the feud was a shared commitment that peace was more important than vengeance. That is always the choice to be made. The organizers of an April 10, 2009 joint Protestant-Catholic commemoration of the Northern Ireland dead, comprised of members of the once-outlawed Sinn Fein as well as their once-avowed enemies, referred to, "the terrible, random nature of death in war and civil conflict." Some lessons have been learned, many more remain.

"*Love your enemies.*" For me, this is one of the high points of Christianity. Rising above hatred has always been seen as a virtue by the wisest of each generation. Martin Luther King, Jr. said, "*Darkness cannot drive out darkness; only light can do that. Hate cannot drive out hate; only love can do that.*" The Buddha said, "*Hate is never conquered by hate, Hate is only conquered by love.*" Because the word "enemy" carries the connotation of mutual hatred, I am inclined to use the phrase, "Love even those who hate you."

You have probably heard the admonition not to judge someone until you have walked a mile in his shoes. Contemplate that, and undertake today's exercise with intention and sincerity.

Today In My World: On today's silent walk, be the person you most despise in the whole world - perhaps Osama bin Laden, or a child rapist, or someone else you find disgusting. As you feel yourself in that persona and feel the stares of hatred from those on the street, what are your body sensations?

Week 3 Day 6: Observing Myself - My Teachers

I am a human BEing rather than a human DOing.
- Anonymous

Our deepest fear is not that we are inadequate. Our deepest fear is that we are powerful beyond measure.
- Marianne Williamson

I honor you and honor all your points-of-view.
- jlh

Who do we most respect and admire? Why our **Heroes** of course. What are the characteristics of a Hero? Heroes are courageous and self-reliant, and they are greatly admired. Being courageous and self-reliant are the characteristics that create heroes. Being admired is something that comes afterward.

Name a genuine Hero who followed the crowd? It's a crazy question, because Heroes don't follow the crowd. A hero may or may not lead other people, but all heroes lead themselves. Heroes are self confident independent thinkers who make courageous choices. By committing their entire focus to their goals, Heroes leave no time or energy for worry or self-inflicted emotional suffering. Heroism is a path to a joyful life as well as to inspired service.

Want to be a Hero, just pick one to emulate - WRONG. To be heroic, don't emulate a hero, learn from one. Heroes don't follow anyone, they set their own course.

Today's exercise will consider your own greatest hero and which of their qualities inspire you. To get you warmed up, let me tell you about my greatest hero...

Y. C. James (Jimmy) Yen (Yan Yangchu): (1893-1990) - Charismatic Visionary, Humanitarian, and Educator

An invasion of armies can be resisted, but not an idea whose time has come.
- Victor Hugo

Go to the people
Live among them
Learn from them
Love them
Serve them
Plan with them
Start with what they know

Build on what they have.
- Jimmy Yen

A leader is most effective when people barely know he exists.
When his work is done, his aim fulfilled, his troops will feel they did it themselves.
- Lao Tzu

My personal Greatest Hero is Jimmy Yen. You have probably never heard of Jimmy Yen - most Americans haven't. Not that he went without recognition. The novelist Pearl Buck wrote his biography. Time magazine wrote about him, and Reader's Digest wrote about him several times - once as a feature article. In 1943, Jimmy Yen received the prestigious Copernican award as one of 10 highly influential "modern revolutionaries" including Albert Einstein, Orville Wright, Walt Disney, and Henry Ford. He also received the Ramon Magsaysay Award for International Understanding in 1960, and in 1983 he received the Eisenhower Medallion of the People-to-People Foundation for his "exceptional contribution to world peace and understanding."

Jimmy Yen was a very unassuming man who never sought personal recognition or glory. He didn't start out with a huge vision, either. His greatest commitments were to his wife, his strong Christian faith, and to the people around him. His immense contribution to humanity began in a very small way, and grew, and grew, and grew exponentially.

In 1918, immediately after graduating from Yale University, Jimmy Yen was swept up into the First World War. He went to France as a YMCA volunteer to interpret for a few of the 180,000 Chinese peasants who had been brought to France by the Allied Forces to work as laborers.

While working among the Chinese laborers, Jimmy found these people to be eager and intelligent, but universally uneducated - that is, unable even to read or write their own name. Jimmy spent many hours reading Chinese language newspapers to these men and writing letters for them to send back to their loved ones in China.

Jimmy wished that he could teach his new friends to read and write, but there was a second reason for these peoples' illiteracy beyond the poverty and exceedingly hierarchal class structure of rural China. Chinese is an extremely complex language that is written using tens of thousands of intricate characters - each representing a complete word, rather than a letter.

Even more confounding for a common Chinese speaker trying to master reading and writing, the language that was read and written by educated Chinese at that time was Classical Chinese, which is not a written representation of conversational Chinese, but rather a formalized language virtually unchanged for 2000 years. It was as if the only path for an Italian to learn reading and writing was to learn to read and write Latin.

In spite of the great perceived difficulties, and the mediocre success that other YMCA volunteers had had in teaching the laborers to read and write Classical Chinese, Jimmy still visualized the laborers reading their own newspapers and writing their own letters home.

As he looked at the correspondence he was writing, Jimmy was struck by how often a very small number of characters (words) recurred. Inspired genius struck, and Jimmy selected 1000 characters that he believed could communicate virtually any idea.

Putting flesh on the bones of inspiration, Jimmy made the decision to teach the writing of Vernacular Chinese (Baihua) - a written representation of spoken Chinese - rather than Classical Chinese. Although there had been a effort to promote Baihua in China for several years, it had not gathered momentum, and Baihua remained virtually unused.

Jimmy offered to teach the laborers reading and writing using his 1000 Character System. 40 of the 5000 men in his camp accepted his offer. The training was so successful that many more wanted to join the next class.

Soon, almost all the laborers in that camp were writing their own letters home, and reading a newsletter Jimmy had printed for them in 1000 Baihua characters. Word spread rapidly, and other volunteers started teaching Jimmy's 1000 Character system throughout the Chinese laborer camps in France.

Jimmy then made a vow to return to his country of birth and educate everyone in rural China.

Jimmy returned to the United States, completed a Masters program at Princeton, obtained financial support from the YMCA-In-China program to launch a Chinese literacy program, and set sail for China with his new bride Alice - who was to become his lifetime companion and committed co-worker in the Literacy and Rural Reconstruction movements.

In 1923, Jimmy established the Chinese Mass Education Movement, and launched what quickly became a nationwide program to teach 1000 Character literacy.

In 1926, Jimmy expanded his work to address the four interlocking problems of ignorance, poverty, disease and civic inertia, with an integrated Rural Reconstruction program of education, livelihood, health and self-government - "integrated, people-centered and sustainable rural development" in his words.

In 1928, John D. Rockefeller Jr. made a large personal contribution to Jimmy's work and inspired many other Americans to do the same.

With the onset of the Second World War, Jimmy came back to the United States to raise funds for reconstruction in China. Jimmy made powerful friends in America - including Eleanor Roosevelt and Henry Ford - and in 1948 secured funding for post-war reconstruction through the "Jimmy Yen Provision" of the China Aid Act.

In 1950, when his work in China was halted by the incoming Communist government, Jimmy and Alice turned their attention to the world, working with rural reconstruction in the Philippines Thailand, India, Ghana, Guatemala, Columbia, Mexico and Cuba.

In 1960 Jimmy founded the International Institute of Rural Reconstruction in the Philippines.

In 1985 the Chinese government finally welcomed Jimmy back to China and acknowledged his immense contribution to Mass Education and Rural Reconstruction in China.

Today, the International Institute of Rural Reconstruction (IIRR), a worldwide organization based in the Philippines, continues the work begun by Jimmy and Alice Yen and serves as a living memorial to their work.

Beginning with the desire to teach a few simple laborers to read and write, Jimmy Yen's life unfolded over more than 70 years of service to directly benefit tens of millions of people around the world.

Best of all for me personally, Jimmy Yen is my uncle. In 1921 Uncle Jimmy married Alice Huie - my aunt and the daughter of my grandfather - the Reverend Huie Kin, pastor of the First Chinese Presbyterian Church of New York City.

For me, Jimmy Yen represents the ultimate in inspired selfless service. Day after day after day, he just did the best he could to take one more small step toward what he believed in. His commitment and enthusiasm were so infectious that people around the world became inspired by his vision.

Exercise: Who is your Personal Greatest Hero? Take pen and paper. Write why you admire your greatest hero, and which of their qualities you want to emulate in your own life.

Today In My World: On today's silent walk, be the person you most admire - perhaps Abraham Lincoln, Mother Teresa, or your Father or Mother. Do you feel proud? Or do you feel an unworthy impostor? What are your body sensations?

Week 3 Day 7: Observing Myself - Peace, Ultimate Blessing

Peace is the ultimate blessing.
- Jewish traditional

Peace begins with a smile.
- Mother Teresa

We shall never know all the good that a simple smile can do.
- Mother Teresa

Every time you smile at someone, it is an action of love, a gift to that person, a beautiful thing.
- Mother Teresa

Ritual is the way you carry the presence of the sacred. Ritual is the spark that must not go out.
- Christina Baldwin

Sense the life force - what the Chinese call 'Qi" - radiating powerfully.
- jlh

Open the gates and roll out the red carpet, for I am entering the kingdom of peace.
- jlh

Choose Inner Peace

Nothing is worth losing your inner peace. Take action as circumstances require, but never surrender your inner peace. Stop. Breathe deeply. Close your eyes and breathe deeply again. Then, and only then, take action - from a peaceful heart.

Today In My World: Take a silent early morning walk. Maintain an attitude of peace toward all creation for the duration of the walk. Focus on your own inner peace. How does it change your experience of the walk to practice inner peace?

Consider taking an early morning walk in silence, focusing on your inner peace, every day next week. Better yet, do it every day for the rest of your life.

Week 4 Day 1: Observing My Interactions - Would I Do *That*?

Stay hopeless and confused. Keep polishing those skills.
- from the movie When A Man Loves A Woman

I can choose peace rather than this.
- A Course In Miracles

He who knows others is wise; He who knows himself is enlightened.
- Lao Tzu

If you want reality to be different than it is, you might as well try to teach a cat to bark.
- Byron Katie

All people know the same truth. Our lives consist of how we chose to distort it.
- the Woody Allen movie Deconstructing Harry

Recognizing my blindness is the first step toward regaining my sight.
- jlh

I am not my attachments - I am not my possessions - I am not the people in my life.
- jlh

This fourth week, we will be focusing on our interactions with those around us - particularly on our interactions with those nearest and dearest to us. This is the hardest part - where the rubber really meets the road.

We see Life through the fun-house mirrors of our point-of-view.
- jlh

We never see Life as it really is. All we can ever see is the reflection of Life - distorted by our unique perceptions.

How many times has each of us listened to a friend's tale of woe, and wondered how they could be so blind. Their stories describe abusive spouses, intrusive in laws, and demeaning bosses.

We hear about their latest romantic interest, and we wonder WHAT are they thinking. "He (or she) is SO wonderful; we just met last week, and already he says he wants to move in with me. He says he's going to get us a house with a white picket fence as soon as he finds a job."

"Gag me with a spoon," we think, "are all my friends ready for the loony farm?" "If I were in their situation, I would never be so blind."

Oh, really? We are always the last to know.

It is one thing to tell a friend what they "should" do to fix their life, but quite another to take good advice when it comes to our own lives. Because we are so close to the situation, we become stuck. We believe that we "need" to stick out the bad situation for financial or commitment reasons. It reality, we are afraid to make the break and start over.

"NEED" is a very interesting word. Really, I don't NEED to have anything or to do anything. I am a being of free-will, and I CHOOSE each and every action I make, every thought I think, and every emotion I feel. Who says I NEED something that I don't want? If I choose to remain in an unsatisfactory job or relationship rather than making the sacrifices necessary to upgrade my career or living situation, I may not be conscious that I am making a choice, but nonetheless, it is a CHOICE.

We disrespect ourselves and our free-will
whenever we say that we NEED to do something.
- jlh

Exercise: Buy a small tape recorder or voice recorder, and carry it everywhere this week. Record all your conversations. It's not necessary to record the other side of phone calls, as the usefulness of this tool is in replaying your own side of the conversation - listening for signs of stress and emotion.

Today In My World: Without trying to modify your behavior, observe when you gossip, complain, interrupt, or have a relevant thought that you fail to share. How does your behavior change when you are stressed?

Week 4 Day 2: Observing My Interactions - Importance

I don't know, I don't care, and it doesn't make any difference!
- Albert Einstein

I think you're the opposite of a paranoid. I think you go around with the insane delusion that people like you.
- the Woody Allen movie Deconstructing Harry

I am merely a bit player in your stories, as you are merely a bit player in mine.
- jlh

Nothing others say or do is because of me.
- jlh

The world is perfect. It's a mess. It has always been a mess. We are not going to change it. Our job is to straighten out our own lives.
- Joseph Campbell

I cannot know what was in Joseph Campbell's mind, but my interpretation is that the world is "perfect" because it exists exactly the way it does. If one believes in a benevolent and omnipotent God, the world is perfect because God created it exactly the way He did. If one is a humanist, the world is perfect simply because it is futile to wish for it be different - and such wishing causes suffering.

Here is another quote that says perhaps the same thing in different words:

The world is perfect. As you question your mind, this becomes more and more obvious. Mind changes, and as a result, the world changes. A clear mind heals everything that needs to be healed. It can never be fooled into believing that there is one speck out of order.
- Byron Katie

Minding other people's business doesn't create happiness for them or for me. In the words of the old saying, "Live and let live." Between living my own life and my commitment to sow a few seeds of joy in the world, my life is quite full, thank you.

Each of us would like to believe that the whole world revolves around us. However, the path to happiness requires accepting that most everything that happens around us, and even to us, is not about us personally.

The second of don Miguel Ruiz' *Four Agreements* speaks to this, *Don't take anything personally.*

Today In My World: Today, whenever someone cuts you off in traffic, or otherwise triggers your upset, remind yourself that the other person's actions are not directed against you personally. You are merely a bit player in their story, as they are merely a bit player in your story. Rather than existing for you only as the driver of the blue Ford, try to imagine them as a three dimensional human being with hopes, fears, pains, emotions, and family, who is possibly driving their feverish infant to the nearest emergency room.

Week 4 Day 3: Observing My Interactions - Why, Why, Why?

Life is what happens to you while you're busy making other plans. - John Lennon
To demand "sense" is the hallmark of nonsense. Nature does not make sense. Nothing makes sense.
 - Ayn Rand

I want to do it because I want to do it.
- Amelia Earhart

I choose to let go of all my attachments. I choose to enjoy people as I enjoy a rainbow or a butterfly - they are most beautiful when they are free.
 - jlh

Human beings want explanations for everything. I don't mean that we go around asking why mice are brown and the sky is blue. Scientists ask those questions, but most of us don't. However, if I ask you right now: "why are mice brown?" you are more likely to explain how it makes them blend with their surroundings, or that God made them that way, than you are to say: "Because they are."

Most strongly and importantly, we always create reasons for our choices. We never state that we did something for no reason at all. Think of Robert Frost's famous poem ***Two Roads Diverged In A Yellow Wood.*** Imagine if instead of "*I took the one less traveled by*", Frost had said "I just randomly took one of the forks in the road, and I got lucky, and my life has turned out well." It doesn't have quite the same ring to it, does it?

Human beings invent reasons for everything! Actually, we invent justifications for everything. Most of the time, we weren't conscious of a reason for doing something before we did it, but we instantly invent a reason if someone questions us, or we question ourselves.

"Why did you go for a walk?" While we may reply snappishly, "Because I felt like it." to someone else asking that question, that is not the answer we give ourselves. We KNOW that we had an important reason for taking that walk. We need to justify taking that walk.

Why do human beings need to invent justifications for their actions? Ah.. another meaningless question. It's just the way human beings are - it's one of the things that defines being human. It's got to do with our primate ancestors, and the phenomenon has been carefully researched using split brain studies - where the left and right halves of a human brain have lost communication with each other.

Monkey Mind is a Buddhist term meaning "unsettled; restless; capricious; inconstant; confused; uncontrollable." Our monkey mind constantly invents stories to explain everything we see and hear. Each human being is the owner an unstoppable monkey mind. Occasionally, we can briefly disrupt our monkey mind before it gets triggered and restarts its story making. Longer term, our only successful strategy for dealing with our monkey mind is simply recognizing its existence, and ignoring its chatter.

Today In My World: After each action you take, or decision you make today, ask yourself why you did what you did. Then remind yourself that whatever you just said was a justification invented by your monkey mind, and say to yourself "I did what I did just because I chose to do it."

Week 4 Day 4: Observing My Interactions - Complaints

Distortion upon distortion . . . the more one uses the mind, the more confused one becomes.
- Lao Tzu

Remember that not getting what you want is sometimes a wonderful stroke of luck.
- Dalai Lama

I've become the person I've always hated, but I'm happier.
- the Woody Allen movie Celebrity

Oh, Shrek. Don't worry. Things just seem bad because it's dark and rainy and Fiona's father hired a sleazy hitman to whack you.
- said by Donkey in Shrek 2

The Answers of Spirit are far more powerful than the Questions of our small minds.
- jlh

We never seem to have what we need. We don't have enough money, or time, or reliable friends. People don't do what they promise. They are late for meetings and keep us waiting. They don't repay their debts to us. Even people we don't know conspire against us. That driver cut me off and then gave me the finger beside - That line at the bank - All those service departments with no service. Everybody keeps us waiting, sells us shoddy goods, and then won't service what they sold us. Nobody respects us or our time. Even our friends don't treat us right. If they were really our friends, we could count on them to help us and sympathize with us, but even our friends never do what they promise. What's this world coming to.

And then there's our job - or lack of a job. We need the money, but we don't need the pressure, the stress, the competition, the schedules, the deadlines, the sarcasm, the disrespect, the bossiness, the control, the lack of appreciation, the lack of cooperation and support, the constant threat of being fired or laid off.

Don't forget the government and "big business." The government taxes and regulates those they shouldn't, and doesn't tax and regulate those they should. Government and "big business" are in collusion to squash the rest of us - or is it government and labor unions - or government and all those foreigners. One way or another, government is all messed up - they're all liars and cheats - if not worse.

Our family is the worst. They don't appreciate us. They don't keep the house clean, pick up after themselves, wash the dishes, or take out the garbage. They turn the TV on high when we want to read, yet shush us when they want quiet. We don't even speak the same language when it comes to sex, God, and how to raise children. We can't live with our family yet we can't live without them. We deserve family we know we can count on - family that always does what we want, and that would never even for a moment consider disrespecting us, let alone abandoning us.

Exercise: Get a BIG box of Kleenex and a cup of tea or hot cocoa. Take a pen and lots of paper to a quiet corner. Write EVERYTHING that's going wrong with life. Focus especially on all the people that are making life a living hell - spouse, lover, parents, children, relatives, boss, co-workers, friends, the anonymous THEM - the drivers in the commute traffic, the bank, the airlines, the doctor's office, the insurance company, the school, the company you work for, the government.

Now stand up, take a deep breath and SCREAM at everyone you're angry at. SCREAM at everyone who has hurt you, disappointed you, failed to do what they should have done, or done what they shouldn't have done. Now, sit down and write another page or two of complaints.

Great Job!! Sorry, you're only half done.

Get ANOTHER box of tissues, refill your tea, and go back to writing EVERYTHING that's wrong with life. This time, focus on all the ways you blame YOURSELF that your life isn't better. Write at least 3 more pages. Visualize being outside yourself and be your own judge and jury. Write all the accusations of fault in the second person, such as: "You are lazy." "Your Father told you that you would never amount to anything, and he was so right." "You're so stupid!" "You'll never have a good job or any money." "You're worthless!" "You're not a good cook, wife or husband, provider, son or daughter, mother or father, student, friend, whatever." 3 full pages. If you need to, stand up and SCREAM at yourself.

Good Work! There is a lot to complain about, isn't there, and we are our own cruelest judge and jury. Take a break now - maybe a walk around the block.

Today In My World: Notice every time you have a complaint. Then notice how the very act of complaining makes you more unhappy than whatever you are complaining about.

Week 4 Day 5: Observing My Interactions - Thoughts

A man is but the product of his thoughts - what he thinks, he becomes.
- Mohandas Gandhi

When you see something done, know that you intended it. If you don't like what you see, then deeply examine your intentions.
- jlh

One day, I decided to drive to the beach for a walk. When I stepped into the garage, I discovered that another car was parked behind mine. My wife had gone off with a friend, and the friend's car was left in our driveway behind my car.

Fortunately, our double garage is long enough that with about ten backings and forthings, I was able to get out through the other half of the garage. I would have said that it took ten minutes, but it was probably really about three minutes to get out. So as far as the actual inconvenience, while I wouldn't have chosen to spend three extra minutes getting to the beach, it was really pretty minor.

However, my first reaction when I saw that other car behind my car was upset. Why upset? A little bit of the reaction was the thought that I might not be able to maneuver my car within the garage to get out. But much more of my reaction was triggered by my story - my story was that my wife didn't care - that she was inconsiderate not to have her friend move her car. And that was my upset.

My upset wasn't having to maneuver my car to get it out, my upset was my thought that SHE WAS INCONSIDERATE. And Suze is NOT inconsiderate - she is never inconsiderate - she is extremely thoughtful, and almost always attentive to details. So this isn't at all about her, it's about my getting tweaked about something ... well, just about my getting tweaked.

So I just observed myself getting tweaked, and... but there is no "and" - it's just about me watching me getting tweaked all by myself - just because I got myself tweaked. It's just human to get tweaked about things, and the only question is whether the upset lasts 3 seconds, or 30 seconds, or days and years, and screamings and divorces.

Why would I bother you with such a trivial meaningless story? Exactly because it IS trivial and meaningless. I briefly judged Suze guilty, and then quickly forgave her. She never even knew that she had been judged and forgiven until I confessed my brief upset.

While we also judge each other guilty of major "crimes," most of our self-imposed upset - our self-imposed suffering - is about issues no more inherently consequential than who should take out the garbage.

Today In My World: For everything I say or do today, I ask myself what my intent is. Is my intent pure?

Week 4 Day 6: Observing My Interactions - Expectations

When you argue with reality, you lose - but only always.
- Byron Katie

You got to be careful if you don't know where you're going, because you might not get there.
- Yogi Berra

Expectations Diminish Joy.
- Anonymous

When you expect nothing, you can receive everything as a marvelous gift.
- jlh

When Dmitri Bilgere (author of *Beyond The Blame Game*) announced that he was getting married, he asked all of us in his community this question, "What ONE PIECE OF ADVICE would you give me and Fawn about relationships?"

What would my answer be? Dmitri and Fawn were getting married for the first time, at an age well past that of the usual first marriage, and they were very intent on the qualities they would create in their relationship.

There are many qualities and attitudes that are crucial to a great relationship: trust, freedom from jealousy, freedom from neediness and codependence, granting each other the space to be themselves, not projecting one's past onto the other's future, and of course unconditional love. But which ONE piece of advice would I choose to bless the couple? Here is what stood out above all the others:

> Dmitri and Fawn,
>
> NO EXPECTATIONS! Marriage will not meet your expectations. You will not meet each other's expectations. Your friends' reactions will not meet your expectations. If you are able to let go of all your expectations and go with the flow, your relationship will have the fresh water, rich earth, and Light it needs to grow into its most wonderful possibilities.
>
> CONGRATULATIONS! Have a long, healthy, and joyous life together!

There is a secret wisdom-of-the-ages that holds the key to breaking our cycle of self-imposed suffering...

The secret wisdom is, *"Life is not supposed to be fair."*

This is not sad news. This is GLORIOUS news! Life is not broken. Nothing is wrong. God has not failed, died, or gone on vacation. The world is working perfectly. We just misunderstood. Somewhere along the way, someone got the idea that life was "supposed" to be "fair," and all the trouble started - expectation, disappointment, resentment, anger - a whole cycle of suffering that began with the belief that life is "supposed" to be "fair."

If you still think that life is supposed to be fair, read *National Geographic* or watch *Animal Planet*. Humans are not exempt from the nature of life.

We admit to our children at a fairly young age that the Tooth Fairy and Santa Clause are fairy tales. Why not prevent immeasurable suffering and confess to our children at that same age that life is not supposed to be fair?

Today In My World: For everything I say or do today, I ask myself what expectations are involved. Expectations are actually demands. What am I demanding of myself, and why am I making this particular demand? What am I demanding of others, and why? By what authority am I making these demands?

Week 4 Day 7: Observing My Interactions - Forgiveness

Forgiveness is an act of self-love and respect.
- don Miguel Ruiz

How unhappy is he who cannot forgive himself.
-Publilius Syrus

Today, I say yes to forgiving. I commit to being for-giving love and for-giving compassion in all areas of my life.
- Sheri Rosenthal

When I am able to resist the temptation to judge others, I can see them as teachers.
- Gerald Jampolsky

Would you rather be right or happy?
- A Course in Miracles

I forgive everyone - including myself. I forgive for my own sake, that I may transmute my resentments into Unconditional Love.
- jlh

Most everything in life is about our point-of-view rather than any absolute. If I say, "Judy makes me unhappy," that's neither true nor false. If I say that my happiness has nothing to do with Judy, that is also neither absolutely true nor false. If I say that I feel unhappy when I'm around Judy, that's a little more objective, but it doesn't address the question of cause.

So why is it important whether we blame other people for our unhappiness (or for our happiness)? It isn't because of philosophy or a need to ponder the meaning of life. It's purely practical. If I choose to believe that the behavior of others determines my happiness, I become a helpless tumbleweed, blown about by circumstances, with no apparent ability to direct my own life. However, if I choose to believe that I am in control of my life, then annoying people, like all other obstacles in life, become just stones in my path - a nuisance, but not a road block.

Whenever I choose to carry resentment and hatred, I am shouldering an immense burden that damages my happiness, and often my health. So what if my resentment and hatred are "justified," they only hurt me, not the person I resent.

The key point is that we do have a choice of how we view the various nuisances on our life path. One choice makes us slaves to circumstances, while the other empowers us and motivates us to follow our dreams - and our happiness.

Forgiveness is especially important in close relationships. The longer you have lived together, the more important it is that you not accumulate resentments that tempt you to call upon them in times of disagreement. Make a vow to keep disagreements limited to the current issue. Avoid sentences that begin, "You always ..." or "You never ..." such as "You never remember my birthday." If something happened long ago, forgive and forget. Even if it happened yesterday, consider granting forgiveness for your own sake as well as your partner's. Forgiveness is especially a blessing upon the person doing the forgiving.

Let today be the day you do an emotional housecleaning of your relationship. Gather up all your old emotional baggage and put it out with the trash. Unlike your grandmother's wedding dress, your leftover emotions are of no value to anyone. Better yet, hold a fire ceremony, either alone or with your loved one. Write each past injury on a small slip of paper and release your attachment to that emotion as you feed the paper to the cleansing fire.

The next four paragraphs are taken from *Simply An Inspired Life*.

> I Forgive Myself with Compassion - I forgive everyone, especially myself, for all actions and all inactions throughout my entire life. I accept that no one else has ever been to blame for either my joy or my suffering. The entire cause of all my joys and all my sufferings is my own emotional response to the events of my life, and I am committed to consistently distinguishing between my feelings about events and the physical occurrence of those events. I declare that everyone who has ever played any role in any of the events of my life is entirely without fault.
>
> I forgive everyone for every "wrong" that I believe they have ever inflicted upon me. I forgive them for my own sake, that I may release the venom - the anger and resentment within myself - and regain my joy and serenity. I have compassion for everyone who has ever been a player upon the stage of my life.
>
> Forgiveness is not a reprieve that we give to someone else. Forgiveness for another's act or omission is a gift that we give ourselves. We are the one who suffers the upset and the anger when we feel that we have been wronged. It is our own blood pressure that rises when we hold on to resentment.
>
> Forgiving others is a gift to yourself, given not because they deserve pardon, but because you deserve the serenity and joy that comes from releasing resentment and anger, and from embracing universal forgiveness.

Those paragraphs elicited an outpouring of heart-rending personal stories, accompanied by the question, "How can I forgive THAT?"

These three comments/questions were anonymously posted to the *Daily Inspiration* web site:

> Reading this brought tears to my eyes. I have been wronged by the ones I loved all my life and I am not sure how to let go of the anger and to forgive them. I want to let go of the burden I have been carrying for so long.
>
> I have been abused sexually and beaten by my father almost everyday, I stood there while he beat my mother and my sister and brother. He even tried to molest my sister. Well, he committed suicide a few years back and it's very hard to forgive him for what he has done, but after reading this, I guess that I can try. It just hurts. I think about it almost everyday. Then I get very upset.
>
> I was sexually violated by my stepfather many years ago and it continued through my whole childhood. The only reason it stopped is because I ran away at age fourteen. How can I forgive someone who said I was a liar? He did it to my 4 sisters and I have no family because they all turned on me for speaking up. I find myself very alone at times and I wonder "Did I do the right thing?"

My response: Thank you for your questions. Life has been very hard on you. I wish it could have been otherwise.

I will attempt to answer your question, "How can I forgive?" The short answer is that your act of forgiveness is for yourself, to enable you to stop suffering.

To expand upon the nature and benefits of forgiveness, let's look first at what it means to forgive. The dictionary tells us that "to forgive" means "to stop feeling angry or resentful toward someone for something they did or failed to do." It does not mean that you believe what the person did was acceptable then, or is now acceptable, or ever could be acceptable.

Forgiveness is about ending your anger. Anger is a destructive human emotion that rots our insides. It causes much of the physical illness in the world as well as untold emotional suffering. Freeing yourself from as much anger as you are holding is like taking a three hundred pound weight off your chest and six daggers out of your ribs.

The better question might be, "How can you NOT forgive?" Forgiveness - forgiveness of all people and all acts - is a sure path to happiness.

So what can you do today to end the resentment and anger, and create forgiveness and happiness? Carrying around three hundred pounds of anger is a little like carrying around three hundred pounds of excess weight. It took years to grow that much anger, and it will take time to shed the anger. Today, hold the intention to be one percent less angry than yesterday. Do the same thing tomorrow. If you can stick to that emotional diet, you will have lost all your anger and resentment, as well as any regrets about anything you yourself did or did not do, in three or four months. I'm rooting for you.

Today In My World: Ask yourself, "What would it take for me to forgive my friends and family - not yet to forgive them for past "wrongs" - but just to forgive them for their actions and speech toward each other today?" Imagine yourself forgiving them. Does that cause you to feel more centered and more loving toward yourself as well?

Week 5 Day 1: Accepting My Past - Early Childhood

It is by going down into the abyss that we recover the treasures of life. Where you stumble, there lies your treasure.
- Joseph Campbell

A man is as unhappy as he has convinced himself he is.
- Seneca

Mistakes are the portals of discovery.
- James Joyce

All life is an experiment. The more experiments you make the better.
- Ralph Waldo Emerson

We are born princes and the civilizing process makes us frogs.
- Publilius Syrus

There's nothing wrong with being afraid. We were meant to be afraid.
- the Woody Allen movie Anything Else

I desire to love myself as I truly am - and to live courageously.
- jlh

This fifth week we're going to turn our focus to our past, especially our childhood. To shine a spotlight on your past, the exercise for this week is to construct an autobiographical scrap book with at least one page for each year of your life. We're going to allocate the first four evenings of this week to constructing your book, and the remaining three to looking for insights as you contemplate your autobiography as a whole.

This is such a powerful exercise that you may want to delay your seven week schedule for a few days in order to spend extra time constructing your autobiography.

In constructing your scrapbook, use photos or drawings along with a little text. Focus on major events, but include something for each year, even if you don't have any photos for the year and your memory is vague.

The first time I did an autobiography, my insights were nothing short of amazing. I was fortunate to have access to photographs from my childhood, as well as from many - but far from all - of my adult years.

One of the techniques that adds to the power of documenting your childhood is writing about each year in the way a child of that age would speak. Thus, on my 4-

year-old page, I wrote, "Mommy, I'm afraid of strangers", rather than some adult psychology about fear. Through the process, I learned the age and circumstances at which my painful habits and fears first appeared.

On my age-3 page I wrote, "I'm happy at home with Mommy. Mommy says I'm a good little boy because I'm quiet and clean. I hardly ever see anyone else because Mommy says other little boys and girls are nasty, and she thinks other adults are scary - both in person and on the phone. Mommy doesn't like Daddy much because Daddy drinks. Daddy is out most of the time, and his breath smells very bad when he is home. I think Daddy loves both Mommy and me a lot, and he is always kind to me, but I don't know why he always has to drink and smell bad and make Mommy mad."

And on my age-4 page, "Mommy is yelling at Daddy - why? What's going on here. Mommy never raises her voice. What can be so terrible that she is so upset? What can I do to help Mommy? I love her so much, and I don't want her to be hurt. I feel so helpless. I don't know what to do. Is Daddy a bad man? It doesn't seem to me that he did anything so terrible, but Mommy is so angry at him. Please just stop yelling and love each other. I need you both to be nice to me, but you're yelling and angry instead. When Mommy is angry at Daddy, I feel that I should protect Mommy."

As you can see, there is a great deal of power in writing an autobiography in one's own childhood voice.

------

mommy
i hold your hand in mine,
until it's ripped away.
the fear, the loss, the world, the cold,
the strange not known, the who unkind.
you put the fear of them in me,
yet you say i must be brave.
i sense your fear when others speak
in ways you would not choose.
within your house you wear the air
of comfort, calm, and joy.
among the world your voice doth quake
and scares your four year boy.
the bus has come. i step on board.
your tears are plain to see.
you tell me not to cry,
and sail me off to sea,
adrift among class, book, and kid
so far away from thee.

Today In My World: Begin your autobiographical scrapbook, focusing on your early childhood. Use events to establish context, but concentrate on reconstructing the emotions you felt at the time, using age-appropriate phrasing. Be sure to include at least one page for each year of your life.

Week 5 Day 2: Accepting My Past - Adolescence

Your thoughts create your reality. Your mind is more powerful than you know.
- Neale Donald Walsch

Fear not for the future, weep not for the past.
- Percy Bysshe Shelly

I'm awash in self-contempt!
- the Woody Allen comedy Celebrity

A Poem of Adolescence
hate to my father, cruel hate,
confused with love - a mix not great.
the man i love - the man i hate;
the man i want to emulate.

the sons of the sons of my sons will say
that hate-love of father has made them that way.
it always has been and always will be,
that i am my father; my sons are me.

Today, we look at our adolescence, the years of hormones and rebellion.

Today In My World: As you continue to work on your autobiographical scrapbook, create pages for your teen years. Look particularly at your conflict with your parents. It is natural to want to emulate our parents, especially our same-sex parent, and simultaneously to swear that we will NEVER be like them.

Week 5 Day 3: Accepting My Past - On My Own

We are just an advanced breed of monkeys on a minor planet of a very average star. But we can understand the Universe. That makes us something very special.
- Stephen Hawking

Tradition is the illusion of permanence.
- the Woody Allen movie Deconstructing Harry

Soon we'll be out amid the cold world's strife.
Soon we'll be sliding down the razor blade of life.
But as we go our sordid sep'rate ways,
We shall ne'er forget thee, thou golden college days.
- Tom Lehrer - song: Bright College Days

I want a girl just like good old mom,
who is different in every way.
- jlh

The girl of my dreams is my mother's shadow,
cast upon the distant movie screen of my future.
- jlh

Today, we look at our late teens and early twenties, the years we leave the nest.

Today In My World: Continue to work on your autobiographical scrapbook, creating pages for the years in which you first lived on your own. Look particularly at your first romantic relationships.

Week 5 Day 4: Accepting My Past - Adult Issues

To manage your mind, know that there is nothing, and then relinquish all attachment to nothingness.
- Lao Tzu

It's not the situation that's causing your stress, it's your thoughts, and you can change that right here and now.
 - Gerald Jampolsky

One minute you're in the lunchroom at Glenwood High and you f***ing blink and you're 40, you blink again and you can see movies at half price on a senior citizen's pass. Ask not for whom the bell tolls, or to put it more accurately, ask not for whom the toilet flushes.
- the Woody Allen movie Celebrity

I'd rather have thirty minutes of wonderful than a lifetime of nothing special.
- from the movie Steel Magnolias

This being grown up isn't all it's cracked up to be.
- jlh

> *I need more more more more*
> *Money money money money*
> *Kids kids kids kids*
> *Stuff stuff stuff stuff*
> *I have less less less less*
> *Time time time time*
> *Joy joy joy joy*
> *Me me me me*
> *Why why why why?*
> *Work work work work*
> *Do do do do*
> *Same same same same*
> *And tomorrow I'll do it all over again.*

Today, look at your adult years. Focus on your challenging adult relationships - possibly Marriage, Children, Job. If you have your own children, perhaps you now understand why your parents were grumpy. In the eyes of their children, parents seldom appear to do anything right.

Parents or other adults who train children, just can't win. I'm not being cynical or sarcastic, it's just the nature of being human. Each and every one of us forces multiple breaks with our adult caregiver/trainers. We are torn between a compulsion to be just like the adults in our life, and another compulsion to rebel and become exactly opposite to the adults in our life in as many ways as possible. Psychologists call this a "Break-In-Belonging," and tell us that we typically experience three especially acute episodes of break at roughly 4, 11, and 17 years of age.

Today In My World: Continue to work on your autobiographical scrapbook, creating pages for your adult years.

Week 5 Day 5: Accepting My Past - Owning My Shadows

What's done is done
- William Shakespeare

My only reason for not experiencing bliss at this very moment is thinking about what I don't have.
- jlh

Do you notice that whatever happens in your life, you tend to feel the same emotions? If you tend to experience anger, you probably have a lifelong pattern of responding to circumstances with anger. Same with jealousy, envy, disappointment, sadness, guilt, or other emotions. People who don't share a particular emotion can't understand how that emotion can dominate other lives. If anger isn't your particular emotion, it's hard for you to empathize with someone whose whole life is awash in feelings of anger.

Current events trigger old emotions. You may believe that you are upset by what your spouse or boss or someone on the street says or does, but there is also a role - perhaps a major role - that past events play in your upset. If you were bullied by schoolmates, molested, shot at in war, or otherwise traumatized, everything you see today is colored by your past experiences.

What to do? If you are extremely traumatized by your past, professional counseling is probably the only course of action that can clear your path for a happy life. If your reaction to your history is the more typical kind, analyzing your autobiographical sketch to look for patterns will provide a great beginning for reconciling with your past.

Be very forgiving of yourself as you identify the patterns of your lifelong behaviors. It took you many years to learn the habits that are now causing you to suffer, so allow yourself time to unlearn those habits. Accept yourself as a magnificent human being while you undertake the project of owning your shadows and learning new repetitive behaviors that bring joy to your life.

Today In My World: Identify the emotions that most trouble you, and read through your autobiographical scrapbook to discover when each of those emotions first developed. As an example, I traced my shyness to specific events in my fourth year.

Week 5 Day 6: Accepting My Past - Un-Learning & Re-Training

Love never dies a natural death. It dies because we don't know how to replenish it's source. It dies of blindness and errors and betrayals.
- Anaïs Nin

Find a place inside where there's joy, and the joy will burn out the pain.
- Joseph Campbell

The remedy for wrongs is to forget them.
- Publilius Syrus

At all times and under all circumstances, we have the power to transform the quality of our lives.
- Werner Erhard

Darkness is not a force - it is merely the absence of light. Observe that when a light is brought to a dark place, the darkness disappears.
- jlh

By nature, we are all creatures of habit. We instinctively adopt familiar routines for most activities. We eat about the same number of meals each day - at more or less the same times. We have a regular pattern of sleeping - unless it is perturbed by illness or shift work. Most everything we do is habitual. Especially note that our attitudes toward people, events, and toward life in general are habitual.

You probably eat three meals each day, but why? Why not two or five? There is nothing particularly "natural" about our pattern of eating three meals each day - it is just a habit that we share with most of those around us. Actually, a number of studies indicate that eating five smaller meals is more satisfying and healthier than eating three large ones.

You will always have habits - things you do regularly and without conscious thought - but you do have the ability to CHOOSE your habits.

1. Create motivation to end the habit.
2. Have patience. You didn't acquire the habit overnight, don't expect to end it on a single day.
3. Cultivate a beneficial habit to replace the harmful one. For example, a daily positive affirmation can take the place of the negative self-talk you want to eliminate, in the same way that chewing gum can replace a cigarette.

These techniques work to end all habits that aren't serving you well, and replace them with positive habits...

1. Begin to pay attention to WHAT you do, WHEN you do it, and WHY you do it. One of the bad habits I fell into was eating a large dish of ice cream in the late evening. Obviously, "ice cream" was the "what," but the "when" was more than just "in the evening." "When" was times I felt stressed, hadn't had a satisfying dinner, or was bored. "Why" was mouth sensation, having something to do with my hands, and sometimes hunger.

2. Keep a journal of the "what", "when," and "why." Make an entry whenever you find yourself doing something that isn't really your choice. You will find that you gain better insight into the "when's" and "why's" as you get more entries in your journal. Soon a pattern will emerge that can enable you to find healthy habits to replace the harmful ones.

3. Look for other activities that would satisfy the "when" and "why." A hot bath for stress, hard candy for mouth sensation, a good book for activity, a warm bowl of soup for real hunger.

4. Make the undesirable activity difficult. Don't keep the cigarettes or ice cream in the house. When ice cream was in my own freezer, it was hard to resist, but when eating a dish of super chocolate chunk required a trip to the convenience store, it was much easier to turn my attention to other activities and a low calorie snack - if any snack at all.

5. Begin new habits not only because you need them to replace unhealthy ones, but also because they are the things you always wanted to do, but couldn't find the time or money. That book club or yoga class makes a great substitute for the eating or smoking, and you can more than pay for your health club membership with what you save on cigarettes.

Today In My World: Identify one emotional habit that is interfering with your happiness, and resolve to replace it with a positive habit. Resolve to replace the negative habit by one percent each day, but handle whatever setbacks you encounter with love and perseverance.

Week 5 Day 7: Accepting My Past - Loving My Real Self

To be oneself is a rare thing, and a great one.
- Ursula Le Guin

Do not dwell in the past, do not dream of the future, concentrate the mind on the present moment.
- the Buddha

You are perfect exactly the way you are.
- Werner Erhard

Do not go where the path may lead, go instead where there is no path and leave a trail.
- Ralph Waldo Emerson

The talent for being happy is appreciating and liking what you have, instead of what you don't have.
- Woody Allen

Be simply yourself and don't compare or compete.
- Lao Tzu

Don't let your past drive your future - choose your life with consciousness today.
- jlh

Love yourself exactly as you are at this moment and you will be happy. There is no reason that you should be any other way than you are. There is no one you must please or obey. You are a magnificent creation, appreciate yourself and express thanks that you are yourself.

While you may choose to continue to learn and to replace habits of suffering with habits of joy, always know that everything you do, or don't do, is your choice, and only your choice.

Say NO to the demands of the world.
Say YES to the longings of your own heart.
- jlh

Do you ever stop to ask yourself WHY you "need to do" something? What is the "need," and on whose authority has the need been established?

We disrespect ourselves and our free-will
whenever we say that we NEED TO DO something.
- jlh

Everything we do is a choice! In every instant, we are making a choice about what we will do in that instant (as well as a choice about what we will think). We may choose to turn off and shut down our conscious attention, and allow the autopilot of our habits and instincts to make our choices, but they're still choices.

I have no need to conform to the stereotypes others have defined for me.
- jlh

Your spouse says "You need to go to the grocery store today," and you say "I need to go to the grocery store today," or perhaps you say to yourself "I need to get a divorce." Look at all the "need to's." Who says so? There is no inherent "should," "must," or "need to" here. There are choices and there are consequences. The consequence of not going to the grocery store today may be eating peanut butter sandwiches or sleeping alone tonight, but there is no "need to."

The world is not going to end because we don't go to the grocery store - and even if the world ending were to be the consequence of our choice not to go to the grocery store today, it's still merely the consequence of a choice that we make of our omnipresent free-will. We have free-will in every instant. Part of that free-will is the free-will to turn off our attention, abdicate conscious choice-making, and repeat "I should," "I must," "I need to" in zombie-like fashion. But don't do it! Love yourself exactly as you are and make all your choices from consciousness.

Today In My World: Be conscious of loving yourself. Remember to say NO to the demands of the world, and YES to the longings of your own heart.

Week 6 Day 1: Transformation - Overcoming My Fears

Every thought we think is creating our future.
- Louise Hay

Intent is what can make a man succeed when his thoughts tell him that he is defeated.
- Carlos Castaneda

If you can imagine it, you can achieve it.
- Anonymous

No pessimist ever discovered the secret of the stars, or sailed to an uncharted land, or opened a new doorway for the human spirit.
- Helen Keller

My greatest Power and my greatest Inner Peace come when I Intend my future, and when I avoid Expecting it.
- jlh

Participate joyfully in the sorrows of the world. We cannot cure the world of sorrows, but we can choose to live in joy.
- Joseph Campbell

What is not love is always fear, and nothing else.
- A Course In Miracles

A warrior acts as if he knows what he is doing, when in effect he knows nothing.
- Carlos Castaneda

Nothing in life is to be feared, it is only to be understood. Now is the time to understand more, so that we may fear less.
- Marie Curie

I lay aside the battles within my own mind, and grant myself peace.
- jlh

In this sixth week, we address attitudes toward life. What is your perspective, your point of view, toward life? What do you believe about the nature of life? Would you be willing to adopt a different perspective on life if it would transform your suffering into joy? This is a week of deep questions and insightful inquiries. Bring an open mind and open heart.

What if you lost your job, your house burned down, the creditors were closing in, and your marriage had become hellishly confrontational? No, that's not make believe. That's the real life of a real person. How can you maintain a positive outlook under such stress and strain?

Here are six ways to find joy in the face of overwhelming circumstances:

1. Start by finding things for which to be grateful. Gratitude is crucial to your happiness. If you are reading this article, you are alive and your brain is functioning fairly well. Start your gratitude list with living, breathing, and thinking. Add every blessing, however tiny, to your list. Every moment without pain is a blessing, every bite of food, every bird, tree, and butterfly. Give thanks for every "hello," and every smile.

2. Give thanks, also, for the life lessons. Make a list of what you have learned - yes, a written list. Be grateful for each lesson. Life lessons often come at great cost, but they are priceless jewels.

3. Do you have a support system - friends and family you can confide in? If so, be very grateful, and use that network now. Don't be embarrassed to seek emotional support from those you respect and love. If you don't feel you have a support network, find one in your church or community, and be grateful for those who are willing to be of service.

4. Care for your body and spirit with special attention and gentleness in this time of great challenge. Several times each day, take a moment to breathe deeply and center yourself. Consider beginning yoga or qigong. Eat healthy, keep hydrated. Get enough sleep. If you have trouble sleeping, pay special attention to the rest of the ideas in this article, they will all help you sleep better.

5. Begin each day with a silent walk: Get up a half hour earlier to make time for it. While a walk in a natural setting is ideal, a walk on city streets will do fine. Thoughts, angers, resentments, and fears will form in your mind as you walk. That "mind chatter" is always with us whenever we are not focused on a specific mental activity, and it gets much stronger when we are stressed. Neither resent the mind chatter, nor let it linger. Say "thank you" to each passing thought, anger, resentment, or fear - then release it and return to your silent walk.

6. Release your angers, resentments, and fears by feeding your troubles and fears to the cleansing fire: Light a candle or small fire. Write one trouble or fear on a piece of paper, and feed it to the fire, while releasing the issue to Spirit. Repeat until you can no longer think of another issue that burdens you.

May your days be bright with joy and hope.

Today In My World: Release your angers, resentments, and fears by feeding your troubles and fears to the cleansing fire: Light a candle or small fire. Write one trouble or fear on a piece of paper, and feed it to the fire, while releasing the issue to Spirit. Repeat until you can no longer think of another issue that burdens you.

Week 6 Day 2: Transformation - Releasing Anger

Holding on to anger is like grasping a hot coal with the intent of throwing it at someone else; you are the one who gets burned.
- the Buddha

Moderating the Anger Response Through Training

You probably can't hit a baseball as well as Albert Pujols. Why? Certainly major league players were born with some level of physical advantage over the rest of us, but most of their skill comes from training - relentless training, year after year. Imagine a baseball coming toward you at a hundred miles per hour - that's less than a half second from pitcher's hand to catcher's mitt. Decide whether to swing. Then decide how to swing. Then actually swing the bat. All in less than a half second. Does Albert think about swinging the bat? I doubt it. That quick a reaction has to be instinctive. Instincts are something we are born with, right? In this case, no. The instinctive response Albert now has to the approach of a fast moving baseball is the result of years of training.

Most people think that anger is an instinctive response, and that some people were just born with the temperament to get angrier faster than others. That statement is half right. Anger is an instinctive response. We respond to an affront with anger in the same time as a pitched baseball reaches the batter - essentially instantaneously - much too quickly for conscious thought to be called upon. But the instinct of the anger response can be trained in the same way as a batter's response is trained - through conscious repetition, visualization, and coaching. Visualization is seeing the event we desire to master in our mind's eye. We see the approaching baseball or the antagonistic action as if it were real, and then mentally practice our response.

During his training, a baseball player strives to make each swing better than the last. The repetition of a faulty swing would be worse than useless. It would ingrain bad habits. The same is true of emotional responses. If we allow ourselves to continue to have the same angry responses, we just entrench our anger habit. But if we strive - through consciousness, visualization, and coaching - to moderate our anger response over time, we can train ourselves to respond to events as we choose, without anger. You can't magically be free from anger tomorrow, but you can put yourself on a training program that will reduce the frequency and intensity of your anger response day by day, year by year.

My training advice for moderating the anger response is:

1. Consciously practice responding with a little less anger each time a situation provokes you.

2. Practice visualizing aggravating situations and rehearse the response you choose to make to such events.

3. Have patience. It took you years to get so angry. It may take years to reduce anger down to a minor twinge.

4. Understand that you can never completely eliminate the anger response. Minimizing anger requires lifelong conscious practice.

The preceding advice is intended for those who are quick to anger, and who display their anger outwardly. But what about people who don't appear to anger? Some people who don't show anger have trained themselves to moderate their anger response, but many others internalize their anger rather than expressing it. While withheld anger may save family and friends from having to endure an outburst, unexpressed anger is even more damaging to its owner than is anger that is verbalized and acted upon.

For those who suffer from repressed anger, there must be an intermediate stop along the path from anger to freedom. First the anger must be expressed. While I believe that most people can significantly reduce the frequency and intensity of their anger responses through the training steps above, overcoming repressed anger is usually not a do-it-yourself proposition. Professional counseling - often including the physical expression of anger in a controlled environment - can reveal and heal the childhood traumas which triggered the lifelong habit of repressing intense anger and hostility. Once a person has become able to express their anger, it becomes imperative to immediately begin moderating that response, with the goal of feeling no anger, either repressed or outward.

The view that there are benefits to anger has become common, but I believe that statements such as, "When anger is channeled and controlled, it can be a catalyst for much positive change," represent a distorted view toward the anger response. The argument goes that if we didn't get angry, we would become pushovers, but the assumption that we can have values and stand up for those values only by getting angry is faulty.

The other view toward anger, with which I totally concur is, "Anger is now known to be quite detrimental to us physically and psychologically." We don't need anger to be assertive any more than we need a stiff drink in order to stand up for our beliefs. As a example, if someone doesn't repay a loan to me, I can be assertive in demanding the repayment, or I can bring legal action to recover the money, at least as well if I am not angry. And more important, I will be far healthier, both physically and emotionally.

Anger is a destructive emotion that becomes instinctive over the years. Through conscious training, the anger response - whether in the form of outbursts or repressed - can be moderated over time, until it is virtually eliminated.

Today In My World: Resolve to be one percent less angry than yesterday.

Week 6 Day 3: Transformation - Problems Are Illusions

Problems are illusions.
- Anonymous

What you want is irrelevant, what you have chosen is at hand.
- Spock in Star Trek VI

That's the secret to life . . . replace one worry with another.
- Charlie Brown in Peanuts

I choose to feel supremely happy at this very moment.
- jlh

How can a problem be an illusion? While the circumstances are real, a situation is only a "problem" if we say it is a problem. We always have the choice to view the events of our lives from other perspectives.

Do you always look at life from the same point-of-view? Consider viewing a situation as another might view it. Look from behind, underneath, from the distant heavens. View the situation as someone of a different religion, race, or nationality might view it. Pretend you are an alien from a distant galaxy - that should be good for a laugh. Troubles only appear troubling to those close to them.

Why is it important whether we blame other people for our unhappiness (or for our happiness)? It isn't because of philosophy or a need to ponder the meaning of life. It's purely practical. If I choose to believe that the behavior of others determines my happiness, I become a helpless tumbleweed, blown about by circumstances, with no apparent ability to direct my own life. However, if I choose to believe that I am in control of my life, then annoying people, like all other obstacles in life, become just stones in my path - a nuisance, but not a road block. Whenever I choose to carry resentment and hatred, I am shouldering an immense burden that damages my happiness, and often my health. So what if my resentment and hatred are "justified," they only hurt me, not the person I resent.

The key point is that we do have a choice of how we view the various nuisances on our life path. One choice makes us slaves to circumstances, while the other empowers us and motivates us to follow our dreams - and our happiness.

Today In My World: Pretend you are an alien from a distant galaxy, or an animal or a cartoon character, and view your life today from their perspective.

Week 6 Day 4: Transformation - Accepting Miraculous Gifts

Ask and it will be given to you; seek and you will find; knock and the door will be opened to you.
- Matthew 7:7

Once doubts are banished, anything is possible.
- Carlos Castaneda

Miracles are the natural way of the Universe - our only job is to move our doubting minds out of the way.
- jlh

Making a list of gratitudes is an exercise that holds renewed power each time it is repeated. One can never be too conscious of everything there is for which to be grateful. So make a gratitude list today... and make another one next month, or maybe next week, or maybe tomorrow. Don't take ANYTHING for granted... start the list with "being alive," and "being ME." List EVERYTHING there is to be grateful for... NO Assumptions! NO Expectations!

While you're working on your list, let me share mine: I'm grateful to be alive and ME in this instant. I'm grateful for everything that has ever occurred to bring me to this moment of being exactly who I am today. I'm grateful to my distant ancestors who survived eons of sameness punctuated by moments of terror... who fought saber tooth tigers and barely survived each winter in order to pass down the genes that make me who I am today. I am grateful to my father's father who sailed from China alone as a young boy in the hold of a sailing ship, bringing my genes from desperate hunger to the opportunity of America. I am grateful to my father's mother and her ancestors who brought their part of my biological inheritance from Holland to "New Amsterdam." I am grateful to my mother's parents who brought their share of my genes from an unhappy Germany to a new beginning in Connecticut. I am grateful to my parents for choosing to bring me into the world - 17 years after my only sibling, and at an age when most couples of their generation had completed their childbearing. Just genetically, my chances of being ME are infinitesimally small.

I am grateful for everything my parents did and didn't do. I am grateful for the unconditional love I received from each of them. I am grateful for the lessons of my father's heavy drinking, and my mother's fear of strangers. I am grateful both for the joy of my mother's generous readings and other attentions to me, and for the pain my isolated early childhood later caused me. I am grateful even for the bullying and other painful experiences of my youth, as each one made me the person I am today. I am grateful for every success and every failure I have ever had... every new love and every divorce... every promotion and every firing... every smile and every tear.

There is simply nothing NOT to be grateful for.

Rainbows and butterflies are themselves beautiful and highly symbolic, but they are also representative of all the small miracles of our life - the little things that are so easy to overlook, yet so awe inspiring when we take a moment to notice and to pay attention.

Give thanks for the rainbows, for the butterflies, for all God's creatures - large and small, for the bright blue sky and the soft fog and the gentle rain, for the tree veiled in the season's first frost, for the baby's laugh, for the touch of a hand and the whispered "I love you."

My own "Rainbows & Butterflies" are the squirrels chasing each other around the apple tree, the deer and her fawn who visit us for the apples, the magnificent hawk who swoops low through our yard, the sea otters at play on the beach, the ungainly yet graceful and serene manatees that once came to swim with us.

Consider these "Rainbows & Butterflies"

* a gentle kiss
* a baby's smile
* the voice on the telephone that says "I'm glad you called."
* the gentle whisper from the other side of the bed, "sweet dreams. I love you."
* a song that touches our heart - whether a sad song, a song of love, or a polka
* raindrops on leaves
* brightly colored glass
* a bird in flight
* a basketful of kittens
* a gentle fog
* a sunset
* a roaring fire
* roasting marshmallows
* the season's first dusting of snow
* fruit and vegetables picked with our own hand

Exercise: What are your "Rainbows & Butterflies?" How often are you conscious of the small miracles that happen right before your eyes? How might your life be more Joyful if you adopted the practice of a daily Celebration of your "Rainbows & Butterflies?" How might that Celebration look?

Today In My World: Make a gratitude list. Don't take ANYTHING for granted... start the list with "being alive," and "being ME." List EVERYTHING there is to be grateful for... NO Assumptions! NO Expectations!

Week 6 Day 5: Transformation - The End Of Suffering

We suffer only until we realize that we can't know anything.
- Byron Katie

Living never wore one out so much as the effort not to live.
- Anaïs Nin

A warrior considers himself already dead, so there is nothing for him to lose.
- Carlos Castaneda

Both the mind and the body are mere tools of the Spirit. Intention creates physical reality.
- jlh

You don't have the power to make life "fair," but you do have the power to make life joyful.
- jlh

"I did the dishes, you need to take out the garbage." "You borrowed money from me, you have to pay it back." "My broker told me the market would go up, and just look." "It's not fair."

All suffering is the result of the expectation that life should be fair. Each of us has a concept of how our spouse, our neighbor, our boss should behave. We also think we know how the world should be, what is good, what is bad, how the natural world should behave, even what God should and should not allow to happen. But life isn't fair!

"Fair" isn't even a meaningful concept. Life is not fair. You can't make life fair. You can get angry. You can complain about life not being fair. You can attempt revenge - perhaps violently. You can inflict great suffering upon yourself in the name of life being unfair. You can choose anger, resentment, revenge and suffering, or you can choose joy.

The magic key to happiness is accepting that life was never intended to be fair, and choosing joy anyway.

Today In My World: Go for a silent walk or sit quietly and contemplate whether you can accept that life is not supposed to be fair. If you can, contemplate the freedom you now have to live a joyful life.

Week 6 Day 6: Transformation - Don't Believe Anything

Believe nothing, no matter where you read it, or who said it, no matter if I have said it, unless it agrees with your own reason and your own common sense.
- Buddha

As for me, all I know is that I know nothing.
- Socrates

Even the truth, when believed, is a lie. You must experience the truth, not believe it.
- Werner Erhard

The words of truth are always paradoxical.
- Lao Tzu

It may seem cynical to say, "Trust No One," but it can actually be a reassuring and positive thought. I am not presuming that others wish you harm. A few may and most don't, but that's not the issue here. For the purpose of this discussion, let's assume that everyone has honorable intentions, and is not doing anything self-serving. Let's further assume that they have your best interest at heart and are volunteering to help you with no consideration of benefit to themselves. This is a bit of a stretch, but it sets the stage for the real point.

In their most generous moments, people are attempting to provide you with what *they* think is best for you. That's a problem. Have you ever been happily curled up on the couch on a Saturday afternoon when there was a knock on your door and several cheerful and enthusiastic people offered to show you their way to achieve salvation? They sincerely believe that they know what is best for you. Apply this thought to everyone in your life from the life insurance salesman to your mother. Under the best of circumstances, they sincerely want to provide you with the advice that they believe will enable you to live the life that they think you should. Disregarding any doubts of their sincerity and ability, the question becomes whether you choose to live the life someone else wishes for you.

Conscious trust is one of the underpinnings of a great life. However, what I am asking you to consider today is the difference between trusting someone's intention, and trusting their ability to know what is best for you.

In the example above, I TRUST that the visitors at my door want the best for me (unless that trust is broken). What I don't trust is that they are a better judge of how I should live my life than I am.

Many of us have been conditioned to trust others' opinions more than our own, and I believe that sort of trust is excessive. This is especially true with regard to authority figures - doctors, lawyers, priests. I trust my doctor's intentions toward me, but I don't blindly follow his suggestions without checking other sources also. He was trained to prescribe a pill for everything, and does it with the best of intentions, but I often choose to trust God's quiet voice inside me rather than my doctor's medical advice.

It is impossible for anyone to advise you on anything without presuming that they know what you *should* want. For example, this article is prompted by my belief that you should want to make your own decisions about your life. But don't trust me on that, it's your life.

Don't decide who to trust, decide which ideas to trust.

Today In My World: Contemplate who you trust to know better than you do how you should live, and why?

Week 6 Day 7: Transformation - Let The Light In

All that we are is the result of what we have thought. If a man speaks or acts with an evil thought, pain follows him. If a man speaks or acts with a pure thought, happiness follows him, like a shadow that never leaves him.
- Buddha

I am a little pencil in the hand of a writing God who is sending a love letter to the world.
- Mother Teresa

At times our own light goes out and is rekindled by a spark from another person. Each of us has cause to think with deep gratitude of those who have lighted the flame within us.
- Albert Schweitzer

It is better to light a candle than to curse the darkness.
- Chinese proverb often quoted by Eleanor Roosevelt

As we work to create light for others, we naturally light our own way.
- Mary Anne Radmacher

Darkness cannot drive out darkness; only light can do that. Hate cannot drive out hate; only love can do that.
Martin Luther King, Jr.

One cannot have a mind that is empty of all thoughts, but one can have a mind that is content with whatever thoughts fill it at the moment.
- jlh

Life is all in the perspective we take on it.
- jlh

Today is a day to look at our life from different and broader perspectives. Today would be a good day to look at our lives from a perspective of thankfulness for what we have and a perspective of wonder at our very existence and the magnificence of the world we live in.

Unexpected events can set you back or set you up.
It's all a matter of - perspective.
- Mary Anne Radmacher

Life can look different from a distance

Put some distance between yourself and whatever is concerning you. Distance in space or time always creates a new perspective.

Get up-close-and-personal

Life looks different when you really get involved.

Look at Life in a Different Light

Shine a bright light on your issues, or turn off the spotlight and take a broader view.

Look from a Different Angle

Approach life from a new angle. Assume nothing.

Pretend You Just Arrived in Your Hometown

We just don't see what is familiar. When we go to a foreign land we really SEE because we don't already ASSUME what will be there. Pretend your community is a foreign land and really SEE it. SEE your blessings.

See Life as Play

Who said that life has to be serious?

See How Blessed We Are

Americans have more comfort, more wealth, and better health than ever before in history or anywhere else in the world. If we are not happy, perhaps we should count our blessings.

Choose to See Beauty and Joy

Much in life can be seen as ugly or beautiful - it's our choice. Why would we choose to see any part of life as ugly?

Choose to Celebrate Life

Choose to view life from the perspective of Celebration. Celebrate family, celebrate friends, celebrate love, celebrate different perspectives, celebrate all of life.

Have a Conversation with God

Conversations with God are very different from the usual nature of prayer. Prayers are commonly only in one direction - the one praying speaks and hopes God is listening. Prayers also tend to focus on asking for specific things or outcomes one wants, rather than seeking to better understand the mind of God.

Some of you already have daily chats with God. Some, like my Mother while she was among us, have a daily talk with Jesus. Others, are sure that the idea of a personal two-way conversation with God is poppycock. For those who have not yet experienced an intimate exchange of thoughts and feelings with God, let me offer a few suggestions for beginning the process.

1. Don't expect a blinding light on the road to Damascus. Don't expect a booming voice offering you stone tablets with the Ten Commandments inscribed. For most of us, the voice of God is very subtle, and can only be heard when we pay attention and listen.

2. Believe. Because the voice of God is usually a quiet voice, the slightest degree of skepticism allows us to dismiss God's message as just a daydream or as the result of something we ate for breakfast.

3. For some, conversations with God occur spontaneously. For others, structure and intent work better. Try the following sequence and see if it helps.

Today In My World: Connect with your Higher Power, if you believe in one.

... Exercise or take a quiet walk for at least half an hour to quiet your body.

... Stand or sit quietly while breathing deeply for five minutes to quiet your mind. If you know Qigong or Yoga, these are even more effective ways of quieting your body and mind.

... In total silence, sit with your back straight, your hands on your thighs with palms upward, and your feet flat on the floor. Raise your head slightly, close your eyes lightly, and raise your eyes. If your eyelids begin to flutter, it is a natural sign that you are open to communication.

... State your affirmation that you are in communication with your Higher Power, and begin your conversation.

For some people, the voice of God expresses itself better in writing. Try holding a pen as you talk to God, and let His words flow onto your paper with as little thought as possible on your part.

Don't be discouraged if intimacy with God evades you at first. You are equally the child of God whether you are able to tune in to a personal dialog with God, or whether stress, worry, and fear interfere and create static on the line. Seek out others who do share intimate conversations with God and let them share with you the comfort they receive from direct communication.

Week 7 Day 1: The Future - Life Is A Grand Adventure

You must be the change you wish to see in the world.
- Mohandas Gandhi

True wisdom cannot be learned in a lifetime, but can be revealed in a moment, for it resides within each and every one of us, and always has lived within each of us.
- jlh

I cherish the uncertainty of life's adventures.
- jlh

Life is either a daring adventure or nothing. Security is mostly a superstition. It does not exist in nature.
- Helen Keller

Life's like Vegas. You're up, you're down, but in the end the house always wins. Doesn't mean you didn't have fun.
- the Woody Allen movie Deconstructing Harry

Twenty years from now you will be more disappointed by the things you didn't do than by the ones you did. So throw off the bowlines. Sail away from the safe harbor. Catch the trade winds in your sails. Explore. Dream. Discover.
- Mark Twain

Do not lose hold of your dreams or aspirations. For if you do, you may still exist but you have ceased to live.
- Henry David Thoreau

Fortune and love befriend the bold.
- Ovid

Mama always said life was like a box of chocolates. You never know what you're gonna get.
- the movie Forrest Gump

All your anxiety is because of your desire for harmony. Seek disharmony, then you will gain peace.
- Rumi

If your tendency is to make sense out of chaos, start chaos.
- Carlos Castaneda

Adventure is worthwhile in itself.
- Amelia Earhart

I ride the storm - cheering wildly. I gather strength from the storm.
- jlh

In this final week, we turn our focus to the future. Think big, envision your inspiring future, and then call that future into being.

Until you can learn to view life as a grand adventure, it's going to scare the heck out of you. Once you see life as an adventure, it becomes a game. You can never win the game of life, but you can have great fun playing.

As William Shakespeare said, "*All the world's a stage, And all the men and women merely players.*" When viewed seriously, life is a cause of suffering, but when seen as a game, life becomes joyful.

Life is a constant opponent, and an overpowering adversary if attacked directly. The successful and happy ones dance lightly with life - a parry here, a feint there - always engaged, but never in the direct line of life's heaviest blows.

Dance Lightly With Life: Life does not have to be a serious undertaking. You will make mistakes, you will feel regrets, and eventually, you will die - so what? Happiness comes from dancing lightly with life - playing hopscotch on the river of life - leaping gracefully from joy to joy while laughing at the threats of calamity - even laughing hysterically at our human frailness when we do fall into the muddy torrent.

> *The moment you start seeing life as non-serious, a playfulness,*
> *all the burden on your heart disappears.*
> *All the fear of death, of life, of love,*
> *everything disappears.*
> *- Osho*

Today In My World: See life as a game. Laugh at life. Dance lightly with life.

Week 7 Day 2: The Future - Just Do It with Courage

Life shrinks or expands in proportion to one's courage.
- Anaïs Nin

Courage is resistance to fear, mastery of fear - not absence of fear.
- Mark Twain

When one has nothing to lose, one becomes courageous. We are timid only when there is something we can still cling to.
- Carlos Castaneda

Courage doesn't always roar.
Sometimes courage is the quiet voice at the end of the day, saying,
"I will try again tomorrow."
- Mary Anne Radmacher

Courage is the ladder that supports me as I ascend from Fear to Unconditional Love.
- jlh

I desire to love myself as I truly am - and to live courageously.
- jlh

As Mark Twain says, "*Courage is not the absence of fear, but the mastery of fear.*"

They don't call it cold gripping fear for nothing. Scared, panicked, apprehensive, afraid, you name it - it hits everywhere at once - tightened shoulders, knotted stomach, shivery cold. The body sensations quickly get the upper hand.

Virtually all humans can recall the experience of cold gripping fear - and the others have short memories. What is that cramp in your stomach, the knot in your shoulders, the cold and shivers? It's the fight-or-flight reaction shutting down your digestive tract, etc., and its been with the human race from the very beginning. It's getting your body ready to either fight or run away from that saber-tooth tiger.

Your body is doing just what it's supposed to have done for the last million years. If our bodies hadn't worked that way, saber tooth tigers would have been better fed, and homo sapiens would be a dead end branch on the evolutionary tree. Those early humans whose biochemistries didn't have a strong fear response became lunch for the tiger, or a trophy head for the neighboring tribe, and didn't pass any of their genes down to us.

So let's thank our fight-or-flight physiologies for having gotten us this far. We can't wish away the physicality of our humanity no matter how hard we try, so let's love our bodies, and our genetics, and our ancestors.

Accepting that our physical fear is an inherently human quality is the first step toward leading a courageous and joyful life. To be courageous is NOT to be without fear - To be courageous is to accept our fear and to act in the face of it.

Once we act in the face of fear, our fear starts to dissipate. Our fear stops having center stage, and starts to shrivel up. Those things that we focus our attention on get stronger, and those things that lose our attention grow weaker. So it is with fear. Once we place our attention on more important things, fear shrivels.

In My World - For Life: Whenever I observe physical sensations of fear in my body - whether Cold Gripping Fear, or just a twinge of what might be called apprehension or concern - I just observe my physical reactions. I don't judge my physical reactions as being bad - they're just my physical reactions. I thank my fear - I give thanks to my body for reminding me that I'm human. I take a deep breath - express gratitude - remember the overarching goodness of life - take another healing breath - feel comforted by Spirit - breathe deeply - exhale *mmmm...* - and give thanks for everything that has brought me to this moment.

Week 7 Day 3: The Future - The Power Of My Word

In the beginning was the Word.
- John 1:1

Every thought you think and every word you speak is affirming something.
- Louise Hay

Be Impeccable With Your Word. Speak with integrity. Say only what you mean. Avoid using your word to speak against yourself or to gossip about others. Use the power of your word in the direction of truth and love.
- don Miguel Ruiz

False words are not only evil in themselves, but they infect the soul with evil.
- Socrates

Don't complain, don't whine, and don't gossip.
- jlh

To change who you are, change who you think you are.
- jlh

For some of us, the world appears to provide only a fixed quantity of each resource - a limited amount of food, of money, of love, of success, of appreciation. In this world-view, each of us is in competition with each other human being for these limited resources. The way to gain more is to beat out others, to be the fastest, sharpest, hardest working - to get to the goal first and grasp the money, the stuff, the "best" romantic partner, the promotion, before anyone else. In this view, life has winners and losers, and one should strive to be a winner.

For others, life is unlimited. Their world expands with the generosity, compassion, inventiveness, and service that they contribute. In this world-view, money that is spent or given away returns multiplied. The more love that is given, the more love returns. The more a helping hand is given, the more hands are strengthened and empowered to help. In this view, we can help each other to all be winners. We can all have food, and jobs, and love, and happiness.

How do You View the World?

Today In My World: Set your intent for visioning your future and calling your chosen future into being.

Week 7 Day 4: The Future - Think Outside the Box

Learn the rules so you know how to break them properly.
- Dalai Lama

Do not speak to me of rules. This is war! This is not a game of cricket!
- from the movie The Bridge On The River Kwai

Rules are mostly made to be broken and are too often for the lazy to hide behind.
- Douglas MacArthur

Damn it boss, I like you too much not to say it. You've got everything except one thing: madness!
- from the movie Zorba The Greek

It's all a game anyway, so just change the rules.
- jlh

When life is like a slippery downhill slope, go skiing and scream "Whee..." all the way down.
- jlh.

Today is your day to dance lightly with life,
invite rainbows & butterflies out to play,
Today is your day to practice whimsey,
watch wondrous cloud animals parade your story,
find a magical white bunny down every rabbit hole.
- jlh

Who made the rule that life has to be so serious? One would think that "life is serious" had been engraved upon stone tablets to judge from how most lives are lived. Get a life, smile broadly, sing loudly, paint your rooms in bold colors, search every rabbit hole for a magical white bunny, have caviar for breakfast and oatmeal for dinner, wear a purple coat with a red hat - dance lightly with life.

If being good isn't working - try being outrageous.
- Mary Anne Radmacher

Most of us seldom let the outrageous part of ourselves out to play. Notice that I didn't say "never," I said "seldom." Halloween is one of those exceptions. While there are certainly many "bah humbug" houses on our street, more than half the houses wear an acknowledgement of Halloween - and nothing about Halloween is NOT outrageous.

Mardi Gras is the other time that momentum builds to express our outrageous side. Both Halloween and Mardi Gras feature costumes - behind which we can hide our "real" identity as we try on our outrageous persona.

What if we like our outrageous side best? We "know" that the "right" thing to do is to suck it up, put the costume and the happy face back in storage for another year, re-dress in our frown and gray flannel suit, and trudge back to job, chores, "responsibilities," and "duty."

Don't play it safe, live full out! Maybe TODAY is the day to put the frown and gray flannel into that dusty storage locker, and start to LIVE. Not just today, but EVERY DAY for the rest of your life!

Celebrate today... Celebrate ME... Celebrate Life... Celebrate Rainbows & Butterflies... Celebrate Whimsey...

Take off your shoes and dance on the beach... Play in the mud... Sing at the top of your lungs... and don't care who hears you.

> *Don't die with your music still inside you.*
> *- Wayne Dyer*

What do you want written on your tombstone? It won't be there if you haven't done it. Start today. If you want "never missed a day of work," go for it, but if you want it said that you "radiated happiness to all around - put a smile on every face - inspired us all to be the best we could be," you might want to start today to lighten up, and start to put happiness - yours, your family's, and your friends - ahead of material success or "achievement."

> *Follow Your Bliss.*
> *- Joseph Campbell*

If you want to do it, do it - TODAY.

Today In My World: Do something outrageous today - just because you want to.

Week 7 Day 5: The Future - Powerful Dreams & Action

Nothing happens unless first a dream.
- Carl Sandburg

If you can dream it, you can become it.
- William Arthur Ward

The future belongs to those who believe in the beauty of their dreams.
- Eleanor Roosevelt

The laughing reach of your dreams is as close as your open mind.
- Mary Anne Radmacher

Powerful Dreams Inspire Powerful Action.
When you can taste, smell, and touch your dream, you can enroll the world.
- jlh

Let's take a step back in time and meet Christopher Columbus.

We know of Christopher Columbus today, 500 years after he lived, because he had a Dream, Charted a Course, and Boldly Set Sail.

Christopher Columbus is, and was, a man of very mixed reputation. While generations of American schoolchildren were taught to idolize him for "discovering" their country, more recently he is noted for being the first to bring to America various infections that killed tens of millions of Native Americans, and also for introducing the European version of the practice of slavery.

In his own time, Christopher Columbus had great difficulty in persuading anyone with financial resources to fund his "crazy" idea of sailing to the Indies (that is, Southeast Asia) to trade for spices. Columbus had no idea that anything but open water existed between Europe and Asia to the west.

Columbus would be no more than a tiny footnote to history except that he made two enormous miscalculations that exactly counterbalanced each other. In preparing plans for a trip to Asia, Columbus' arithmetic was faulty, and he severely miscalculated the circumference of the earth. His calculations indicated that the earth was much smaller than it actually is, and that a sailing ship could carry enough provisions to sail westward from Europe to Asia.

If Columbus had calculated correctly, he would have determined that his ships could not carry enough food to sustain a voyage from Europe to Asia and he would never have set sail. As an aside, several potential patrons turned down the idea of funding

Columbus' expedition after their own mathematicians recognized Columbus' erroneous calculation.

Columbus' other enormous miscalculation, of course, is that the American continents were between Europe and Asia. By pure random chance, Columbus reached America exactly the distance from Europe that he expected to reach Asia, and just before his food ran out. If there had been, as Columbus believed, no land between Europe and Asia, Columbus and all his men would have starved long before they reached Asia.

What is the point of this story?

What does Columbus have to do with our dreams?

Like Columbus, we have Dreams that run through our head like full color movies, pleading with us to take action.

Like Columbus, we have many people telling us that our dreams are "crazy," and we should settle for less.

Like Columbus we are unable to anticipate what the future will bring, and what the consequences of taking action on our Dreams might be.

Will we, like Columbus, chart the best course we are able, given the information we have access to at the time, and set sail? Or will we trash our Dreams into the box labeled "fantasy discard pile," and return to doing what others expect of us?

Stand tall, breathe deep, and Choose today to chart the course that will transform your Dream into reality.

Today In My World: Set aside an hour. Find a quiet comfortable place, and create an image, a dream, of a future that inspires you. Let your vision of the future run like a full color movie with surround sound. Make the experience so real that you can taste it and smell it. Let that goal drive your plans and your action. You can create your own inspiring future.

Week 7 Day 6: The Future - Everything Is One

All things share the same breath - the beast, the tree, the man... the air shares its spirit with all the life it supports.
- Chief Seattle

If you want others to be happy, practice compassion. If you want to be happy practice compassion.
- Dalai Lama

Simply see that you are at the center of the universe, and accept all things and beings as parts of your infinite body. When you perceive that an act done to another is done to yourself, you have understood the great truth.
- Lao Tzu

See God in every person, place, and thing, and all will be well in your world.
- Louise Hay

Drop the sword - for there is but one flesh to wound, and it is the one flesh of all humankind.
- jlh

The Divine is all in the perspective we take on it.
- jlh

Today is a day to look at our beliefs from different and broader perspectives. What are our values, and what is our viewpoint toward Spirit and toward Unity with All Creation? Visualize a panorama of children from all nations, all colors, all religions. Do you find some "better" than others, or are we all one?

> *I wrap the potential for bitterness, resentment, martyrdom*
> *in the blanket of forgiveness and just set it down.*
> *Then it just melts in the warmth. And goes away.*
> - Mary Anne Radmacher

Choose to view the Divine and All of Life from the perspective of Celebration. Celebrate family, celebrate friends, celebrate love, celebrate different perspectives, celebrate all of life.

Today In My World: Contemplate the unity of everything. Feel a bond with every person in your extended family, your community, your country, the entire world. Feel a kinship with the animals, the plants, the earth itself, and with Spirit.

Week 7 Day 7: The Future - Life Is a PERFECT Mess

The world is perfect. It's a mess. It has always been a mess. We are not going to change it. Our job is to straighten out our own lives.
- Joseph Campbell

I cannot know what was in Joseph Campbell's mind, but my interpretation is that the world is "perfect" because it exists exactly the way it does. If one believes in a benevolent and omnipotent God, the world is perfect because God created it exactly the way He did. If one is a humanist, the world is perfect simply because it is futile to wish for it be different - and such wishing causes suffering.

Here is another quote that says perhaps the same thing in different words:

The world is perfect.
As you question your mind, this becomes more and more obvious.
Mind changes, and as a result, the world changes.
A clear mind heals everything that needs to be healed.
It can never be fooled into believing that there is one speck out of order.
- Byron Katie

I say all that happens is wonderful.
- Anaïs Nin

The only thing that makes life possible is permanent, intolerant uncertainty: not knowing what comes next.
- Ursula LeGuin

What I recognized is that you can't put it together. It's already together, and what you have to do is experience it being together.
- Werner Erhard

We are powerless to redesign the world, but we have infinite power to design our appreciation of it.
- jlh

Know nothing - for to know nothing is to know everything.
- jlh

The phrase "live and let live" is so familiar that it fails to carry the profound impact it deserves. Much of the true wisdom of life is captured in this simple saying. It addresses the rights of others to their own beliefs and actions, as well as a warning about meddling in the affairs of others.

Let today be a day to honor and respect the beliefs and lifestyles of your extended family, your friends, your neighbors, your fellow citizens, and all those around the world.

It is not our place to know the mind of God. We are not in a position to know what is best in the long run - best for us individually, or best for humanity as a whole. This is often very difficult to accept when we see war and disease in the world and experience physical and emotional suffering in ourselves, our family, and our friends. This belief in God's infinite power and ultimate wisdom is the true test of faith.

Let today be the bridge between the past, regarding which we unconditionally accept that everything has occurred according to God's plan, and a future where we place our unconditional trust in God's omnipotence and His benevolent design for our lives.

What's done is done.
- William Shakespeare

Shakespeare is talking about acceptance. The facts of the past can never be changed. What we can choose is how we view those facts and whether we allow them to corrupt our future. Whatever happened, you did the best you could, given the knowledge and abilities you had at the time. Tomorrow is a new day. Begin with a fresh outlook that does not project your past into your future.

Today In My World: For everything that you see or hear, ask yourself whether you have the ability to make a positive impact, and whether you have a strong commitment to make such an impact. If the answer to both questions is "yes," take action. Otherwise, take a deep breath and completely release the subject forever.

Conclusion - What's Next?

And the day came when the wish to remain tight in a bud was more painful than the risk it took to blossom.
- Anaïs Nin

Lord, make me an instrument of thy peace.
- St Francis of Assisi

The Joy is in the Journey.
- Anonymous

Let me bring Peace into moments of chaos.
- jlh

Bless everything that has occurred to bring me to this instant.
- jlh

I have compassion for everyone who has ever been a player upon the stage of my life.
- jlh

Live as if you were to die tomorrow. Learn as if you were to live forever.
- Mohandas Gandhi

A good traveler has no fixed plans, and is not intent on arriving.
- Lao Tzu

Imagine all the people living life in peace. You may say I'm a dreamer, but I'm not the only one. I hope someday you'll join us, and the world will be as one.
- John Lennon

Do not let your fire go out.
- Ayn Rand

Out beyond ideas of wrongdoing and rightdoing,
there is a field. I will meet you there.
- Rumi

We shall find peace. We shall hear angels.
We shall see the sky sparkling with diamonds.
- Anton Chekhov

Know first that you have absolutely no power to change the world, and then address all your energies and intent toward improving it.
- jlh

My greatest service to others is living happily, and radiating happiness and joy to those around me.
- jlh

ATD: Accept - Transform - Design

Over the past seven weeks, you have done only three things, but if you have done them with courage and an open mind, your life is forever transformed. You have accepted your past, transformed your present attitudes, and begun to design your future with intent.

Accepting Your Past

You accepted that the events of the past cannot be altered. Like everyone else at every other moment of history, you did the best you could at each instant. You can't go back and replay your actions.

What you can do, and what gives you immense freedom and comfort, is to:

1. Recognize that the person you were in your past was not the person you are today, and that younger you did the very best that they could, given the knowledge, emotions, and prior experience they had to draw upon at the time.

2. Create a new and more loving story to explain each event in your past. Remember that neither story is what a video camera would have recorded, so neither story is either more accurate or "better" than the other story. The difference is that one story causes you to suffer, while the other brings you to inner peace. Choose inner peace.

3. Forgive everyone for every "wrong" that you think they ever inflicted upon you. Forgive them for your own sake, that you may release the venom - the anger and resentment within yourself - and regain your joy and serenity. Have compassion for everyone who has ever been a player upon the stage of your life

4. Forgive yourself completely. Forgive yourself for having created a story of suffering. Forgive yourself for all your angers, resentments, jealousies, and all the other emotions of suffering. Have unbounded compassion for yourself at all times and under all circumstances.

5. Give thanks for everything that has occurred to bring you to this moment in time. Every event that has ever occurred in your life has played a crucial role in delivering you to this instant. Have Gratitude for Everything that has brought you to this moment.

Transforming Your Present Attitudes

You have transformed your attitudes toward your emotions. First you observed your emotions in action. You observed conversations and interpersonal interactions in which you were not a participant, and noticed the emotions of the others. You also observed how the conversations and interactions triggered your own emotions.

With this background, you were then ready to successfully observe your own emotions while you were actively participating in conversations and interpersonal interactions. You noticed that you unconsciously invent stories to explain everything you do, say, and think, and then experimented with intentionally creating happier stories to accompany everything you do, say, and think.

You examined the emotions associated with words of suffering, such as: anger, fear, jealousy, expectation, control, ego, dependency, and scarcity. You learned to recognize the physical manifestations of these emotions - tight shoulders, cramping stomach, chills, etc. - in your own body. Having brought focus to those emotions, you were able to accept that having those emotions will always be a part of the human condition.

When you recognize that you are experiencing one of those emotions, thank the emotion for its role in enabling our ancestors to survive prehistoric times and pass on the genes for these unpleasant, and now generally counterproductive, emotions. Then forgive yourself for fighting against the emotion, and consciously invent a happier story designed to trigger a more pleasant emotional reaction. Once you change the story, your emotion will change itself. Understand that it is futile to attempt to change your emotion by shear will power. "I will be happy, I will be happy, I will be happy" just doesn't work.

Gradually building on these exercises and insights, you have reached a level of mastery where you can alter your own emotions and attitude - not directly, and not instantly, but more and more reliably and predictably. Over time, your mastery will grow until you can transform your own emotions in seconds, rather than minutes or hours.

I am the master of my emotions -
I transform fear to love, anger to compassion,
pain to comfort, scarcity to abundance,
expectation to gratitude, and jealousy to generosity.
- jlh

Designing Your Future With Intent

Having mastered your past and your emotions, you turned your attention to your future. While you can transform your relationship with your past, you cannot alter the physical events which have occurred. While you can transform your relationship with your emotions and indirectly choose happier ones, you cannot escape the "fight or flight" or other instincts that kept our cave dwelling ancestors from extinction.

Your future, however, is within your power to choose. You can choose which actions you wish to take, and what you choose to say, as well as choosing the emotions and attitudes you bring to your future.

You have mastered the art of transforming your dreams - your vision of your future - into a tangible reality. You started by expanding your dream for your future, and now visualize your future as a grand adventure to be lived courageously. Nothing BIG comes from dreaming small - to paraphrase the Bill Clinton quote.

You examined the limits that convention and society are desperately trying impose on your future. Choose to break away - breaking the rules of convention, thinking outside-the-box, and spreading your newly found wings.

You found the power of visualizing your dream on the BIG SCREEN of your imagination - feature-length, full color, three-dimensional, rich resonant sound, all the details in place, great supporting cast, and your credits as producer, director, and STAR.

What remains is to use your intent to project your dream onto the giant movie screen of your future. Consider enrolling a supporting cast of enthusiastic teammates for the project.

Powerful Dreams Inspire Powerful Action.
When you can taste, smell, and touch your dream, you can enroll the world.
- jlh

Remember that the joy is in the journey. Here it gets a little like a Zen Koan (paradox) - a riddle which has no answer, but rather, is intended to inspire insight. Living a fulfilling life of joy and serenity is a function of following your dream, rather than of achieving it. Yet, in paradoxical fashion, if you are not truly intent upon achieving your dream, the path of following your dream loses its meaning.

The secret lies in following your dream with inspired intensity, while at the same time, gratefully accepting all the detours and new openings that life provides.

Thank you for completing this training program. I look forward to having you join me in further training and at *Daily Inspiration - Daily Quote* - **www.DreamThisDay.com**

Thank you for sharing with me this journey we call Life,
- Jonathan Lockwood Huie
jlh@jlhuie.com

Simply An Inspired Life:
Consciously Choosing Unbounded Happiness in Good Times and Bad
by Jonathan Lockwood Huie and Mary Anne Radmacher

Are you unhappy, or worried about the future? Does it seem that the whole world is conspiring against you? Your boss? Your spouse? Your family? The government? The economy?

It is possible to enjoy a happy life, even in the face of life's most challenging circumstances. Let *Simply An Inspired Life* be your guide to a joyful life - your beacon of hope in a troubled and confusing world.

Take time out to pamper your mind and spirit. This is the perfect self-awareness book to help you to see and be grateful for what is good in life. Tips, techniques, feel-good stories, and uplifting quotes will make your days more joyful.

"*Simply An Inspired Life* comes to the rescue. It offers not just permission to slow down and get a life, but clear instructions on how to do just that."
- Victoria Moran, author of *Living a Charmed Life: Your Guide to Finding Magic in Every Moment of Every Day*

"Jonathan and Mary Anne remind us that life is so much more than work, school, making money, paying bills -- there are rainbows after the rain, there is sunlight that lights our path, there is laughter and smiles, there are the first steps of a child, there are so many beautiful things to focus on." - a reader

Life change comes about in two complementary ways - the "aha" moment, which occurs in a flash of insight, and the conscious redesigning of our habitual behaviors, which is a lifelong project. *Simply An Inspired Life* addresses both the flash of insight that suffering is optional, and the structural pillars that support living an inspired life.

Chapter two describes a powerful technique for personal transformation called "Breaking the Cycle of Self-Inflicted Suffering". The reader is gently guided through identifying the relationship of perceived scarcity to suffering, and then coached in breaking that painful cycle.

The remainder of the book introduces and develops the Eight Points that are the pillars of Simply An Inspired Life.

Eight Points of An Inspired Life - Keys to Happiness

* HONOR for true self.
* FORGIVENESS for self and all.
* GRATITUDE in everything.
* CHOICE with open mind and heart.
* VISION with powerful intention.
* ACTION with bold courage.
* CELEBRATION with joy.
* UNITY with all creation.

Read more about *Simply An Inspired Life* and order at www.SimplyAnInspiredLife.com or from your favorite bookseller.

100 Secrets for Living a Life You Love:
Finding Happiness Despite Life's Roadblocks
by Jonathan Lockwood Huie

You can live the life you love - even in the face of the most challenging circumstances. While sometimes it may appear that life throws more obstacles in your path than you can handle, you can always choose to be happy. Yes, you are that powerful.

The "secrets" include...
- 1 - Put Your Faith in Attitude, Not Circumstances
- 4 - Persevere - Happiness is Not Always an Easy Choice
- 6 - Give the Gift of Happiness to Your Friends and Family
- 11 - Choose the Purpose of Your Life
- 24 - Stop Anger Before It Stops You
- 36 - Consider How You Want to be Remembered
- 39 - Create Good Endings - They Precede Good Beginnings
- 41 - Put Your Dreams Into Action
- 42 - Gather Strength From Life's Storms
- 44 - Have Gratitude for ALL of Life
- 45 - Be Open to Receiving Unlimited Abundance
- 56 - Give and Receive Love and Compassion
- 57 - Look for the Best in People
- 67 - Make Peace with Your Past through Forgiveness
- 70 - Learn the #1 Secret of Great Relationships
- 77 - Find Happiness Beyond the Grief of Divorce
- 88 - Begin the Practice of a Silent Daily Walk
- 90 - Know That Life is NOT SUPPOSED to be Fair
- 100 - Feel Unity with Spirit and All Creation

Read more about *100 Secrets for Living a Life You Love* and order at...
www.dreamthisday.com/secrets-life-love

------ NOTES ------

Happiness depends upon ourselves
- Aristotle

------ NOTES ------

I give thanks for both my bloom and my thorns.
- Jonathan Lockwood Huie

------ NOTES ------

> **Today is your day to paint life in bold colors,
> set today's rhythm with your heart-drum,
> walk today's march with courage,
> create today as your celebration of life.**
> - Jonathan Lockwood Huie

painting by Suze Stewart

NOTES

> Hate is never conquered by hate,
> Hate is only conquered by love.
> – the Buddha

------ NOTES ------

> *Always be a first-rate version of yourself, instead of a second-rate version of somebody else.*
> – Judy Garland

------ NOTES ------

> *May your spirit soar throughout
> the vast cathedral of your being.
> May your mind whirl
> joyful cartwheels of creativity.
> May your heart sing
> sweet lullabies of timelessness.*
> – Jonathan Lockwood Huie

------ NOTES ------

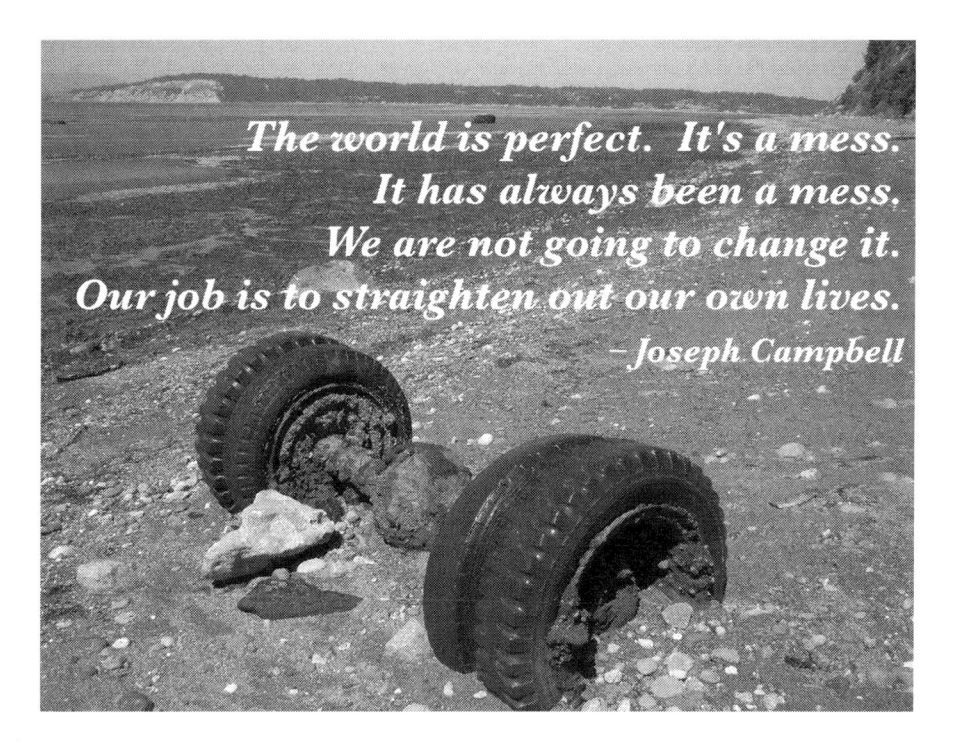

> The world is perfect. It's a mess.
> It has always been a mess.
> We are not going to change it.
> Our job is to straighten out our own lives.
> — Joseph Campbell

------ NOTES ------

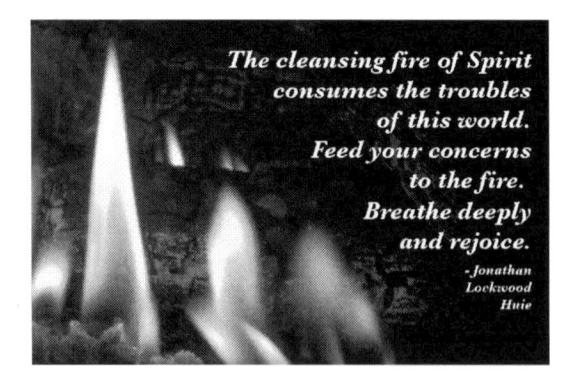

> *The cleansing fire of Spirit consumes the troubles of this world. Feed your concerns to the fire. Breathe deeply and rejoice.*
> —Jonathan Lockwood Huie

------ NOTES ------

------ NOTES ------

> *Standing in the inspiring vision of my future, I boldly take every step - large and small - with courage and intent.*
> *- Jonathan Lockwood Huie*

------ NOTES ------

> *The purpose of our lives is to be happy*
> - Dalai Lama

painting by Suze Stewart

------ NOTES ------

Dance Lightly With Life

Today is your day to
dance lightly with life,
sing wild songs of adventure,
soar your spirit,
unfurl your joy.
- *Jonathan Lockwood Huie*

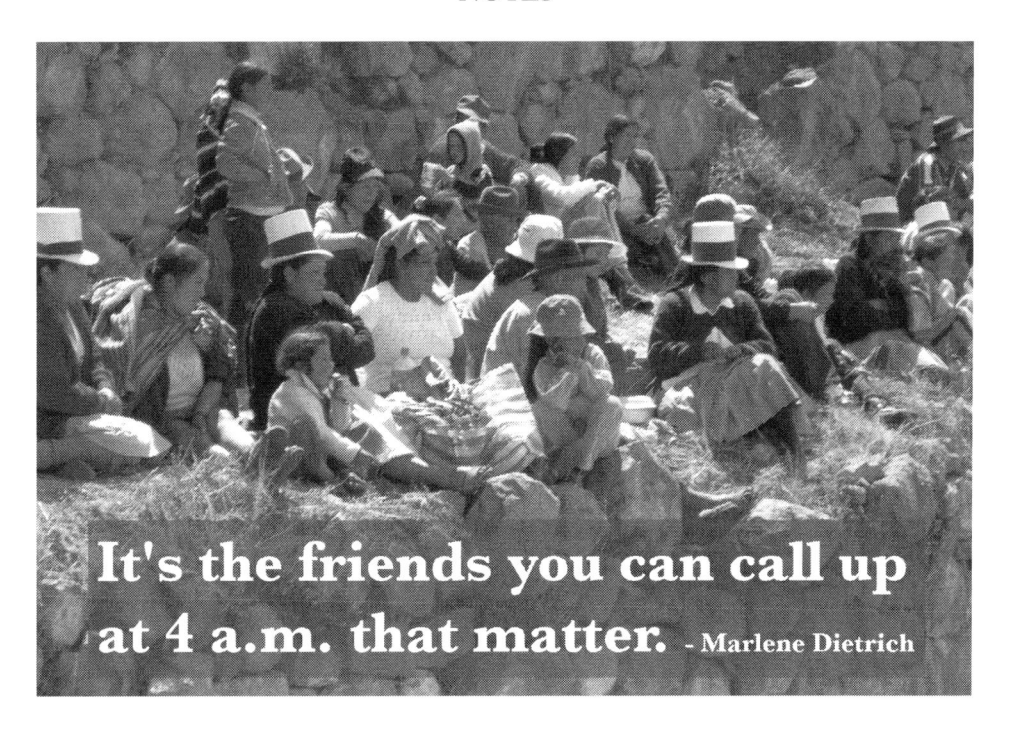

------ NOTES ------

It's the friends you can call up at 4 a.m. that matter. - Marlene Dietrich

------ NOTES ------

There are only two ways to live your life. One is as though nothing is a miracle. The other is as though everything is a miracle. - Albert Einstein

> *Try a new perspective on diversity. Across the country and around the world, we are all one.*
>
> *- jonathan lockwood huie*

Celebrate endings - for they precede new beginnings
- Jonathan Lockwood Huie

Printed in Great Britain
by Amazon